PRESTON IN FOCUS

by

Stephen Sartin

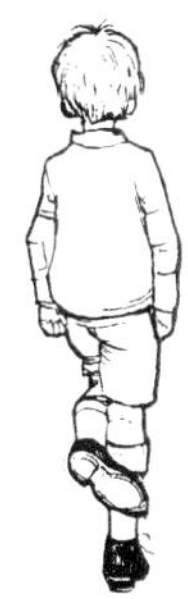

Landy Publishing
2002

ISBN 1 872895 59 X

British Library in Cataloguing Publication Data.
A catalogue record of this book is available from the British Library.

Layout by Mike Clarke. *Tel/Fax: 01254 395848*
Printed by Nayler the Printer Ltd., Accrington. *Tel: 01254 234247*

Landy Publishing have also published:

Blackburn in Focus by Alan Duckworth and Jim Halsall
Blackburn in Times Gone By by Jim Halsall
Blackburn Tram Rides by Jim Halsall
A Blackburn Childhood in Wartime by Marjorie Clayton
Accrington Observed by Brian Brindle & Bob Dobson
Accrington's Public Transport by Robert Rush
Accrington's Changing Face by Frank Watson & Bob Dobson
Bolland Forest & the Hodder Valley by Greenwood & Bolton
Cockersand Abbey by Brian Marshall
The History of Pilling by F. J. Sobee

A full list is available from:

Landy Publishing
'Acorns' 3 Staining Rise, Staining, Blackpool, FY3 0BU
Tel/Fax: 01253 895678

Introduction

When Jim Halsall volunteered to list a box of photographic negatives in Blackburn Library, he could not have envisaged the treasure he would come upon. Tightly packed in envelopes were one thousand five hundred quarter-plate glass negatives which had never been touched since they were stored away ninety years ago. They were taken for a photographic company founded by a Blackburn photographer, John William Shaw (c. 1848-1940). Shaw had been born in Norfolk, the son of an agricultural labourer, but by the 1860s was living with his father at Feniscowles. Interested in the new art of photography, which had only been established some twenty years previously, he set up a studio in Whalley New Road. He prospered, and by 1903 had moved to Preston New Road, where he was joined by his son, Alfred (c. 1874-1954). By the end of the decade, the Shaws, father and son, had diversified their photographic business and were postcard publishers.

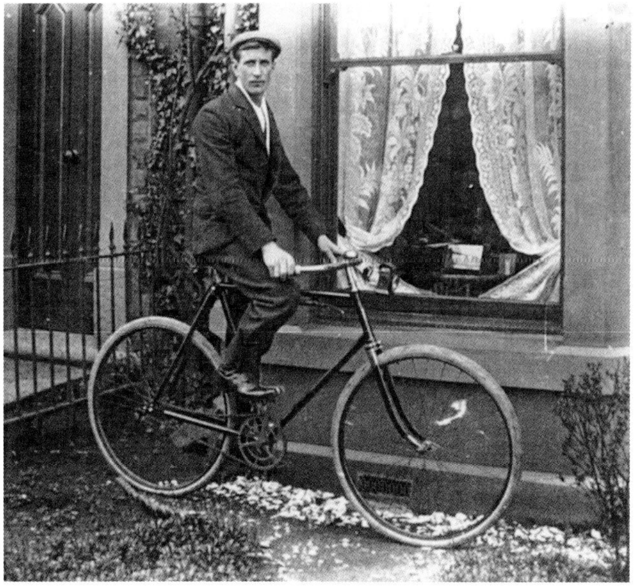

Alfred Shaw was a keen cyclist.

It is not known whether the Shaw photographic archive survived in its totality in the later years of the firm. Perhaps glass negatives of portraits and groups, which would have been of little interest to anyone other than the sitters and would have taken up most of the storage space, were regularly cleared out when it was considered that they would no longer be required. Another possibility is that at the time of Alfred's death in 1954, the date of the donation to Blackburn Library, someone considered that it was the postcard scenes that would have a lasting historical interest. Or, even more likely, the negatives are a fraction of a larger collection that included many other postcard views, and have only survived by chance. Whatever the truth, those remaining constitute an archive of views of the Yorkshire Dales, the South Lakes, Derbyshire, Nottingham, Sheffield, Burnley, Clitheroe, Ribble Valley, Blackburn and Preston, which is of national significance.

Evidence provided by architectural details in the photographs suggests that the surviving Preston negatives date from 1911-12; all the named shop fronts indicate that they were taken about that time. This is confirmed in one of the photographs by a billboard outside a Church Street newsagents, which reads *'Arsenic poisoning tragedy: sensational development'*, which surely must refer to events leading up to the trial of the notorious murderer, Frederick Seddon, in March 1912. In addition, a postcard of Preston Royal Infirmary, with the Shaw negative No. 29, as in the view in this booklet, has a postmark for July 3, 1912.

Then there is the question of who took the photographs. On the basis that they date from 1911-12, John William Shaw would have been about 63, and Alfred Shaw, 37. By the Edwardian era, Alfred was playing the leading role in the Shaw photographic business. The *'West End Series'* postcards published by them carry the name *'A.E. Shaw, Blackburn'*. We may reasonably be certain, therefore, that Alfred was the photographer at that time.

An interesting question is the degree of artifice in the Shaw photographs. It is well known that some postcard companies arranged for well-dressed actors to be in place when the shutter clicked, in order to ensure an aesthetically pleasing though not necessarily honest picture! Alfred Shaw, like so many others taking picture postcard views, must often have contrived to include eye-catching local figures in the near foregrounds of his pictures, perhaps even asking them to pose or play out a part. Could this have happened in the case of the woman scrubbing a step in a view of St. Paul's Road; the two young children standing at Moor Park Gates in Garstang Road; and the two youths standing with a child in a pram at the corner of Deepdale Road and Ribbleton Lane? But what of his photograph of Fishergate with the Old Town Hall, which shows a cyclist and his friend adjusting a bicycle chain outside the headquarters of Preston Cycling Club. The inclusion of this *'incident'* makes the picture one of the most outstanding ever taken of Preston. Whether they are there by accident or design we shall never know. Only Alfred Shaw knew the truth.

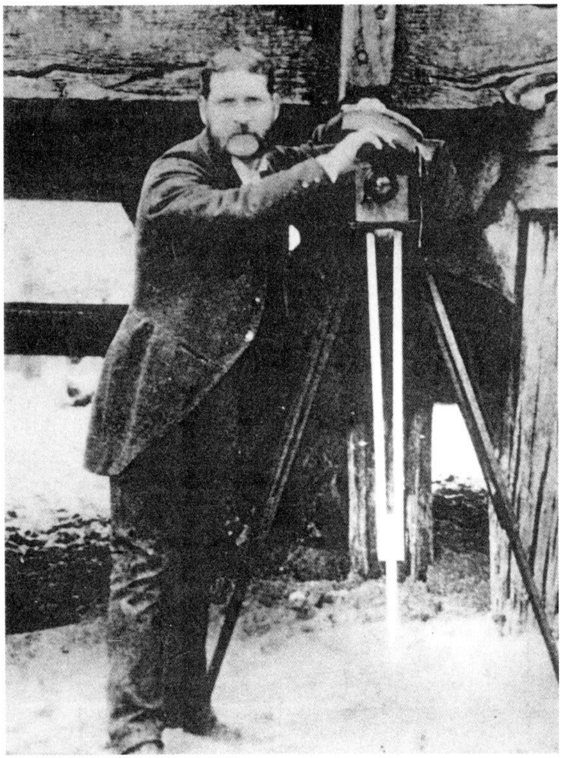

John William Shaw, possibly taken by his son Alfred.

Many people have assisted me in the preparation of this book. I thank Alan Duckworth, the Community History Librarian at Blackburn Library, for allowing me to draw on his knowledge of John William and Alfred Shaw, who took these magical photographs. Thanks are due to Brian Swarbrick, Ray Smith, Ron Severs, John Higginson and Albert Clayton, all members of the Red Rose Picture Postcard Club. To Jim Halsall goes the credit for volunteering to identify and list the collection of negatives, and also for making the photographic prints for this publication.

Such a work as this, which offers a comprehensive picture of Preston, has needed supporting information from several different sources. I thank David Shuttleworth, Reference Librarian, and his colleagues Ann Dennison, Andrew Walmsley, Roger Schultz and Claire Sutton, at the Harris Reference Library, who have been so very helpful.

I thank David Blake for supplying me with information about the trams and early motor vehicles. The help given to me by Madeleine Deane, Veda Gordon, Ellen Emerson, Marjorie Amriding and Teresa Harrison, has been much appreciated. A debt of gratitude is owed to Ian Sutton, Information Development Services Manager and to Diana Rushton, Community History Manager, at Blackburn Library for giving permission for the photographs to be reproduced.

Lastly, I thank Elizabeth Horn for reading my notes, offering helpful suggestions, and producing the finished copy for the printer.

Stephen Sartin
September 2002

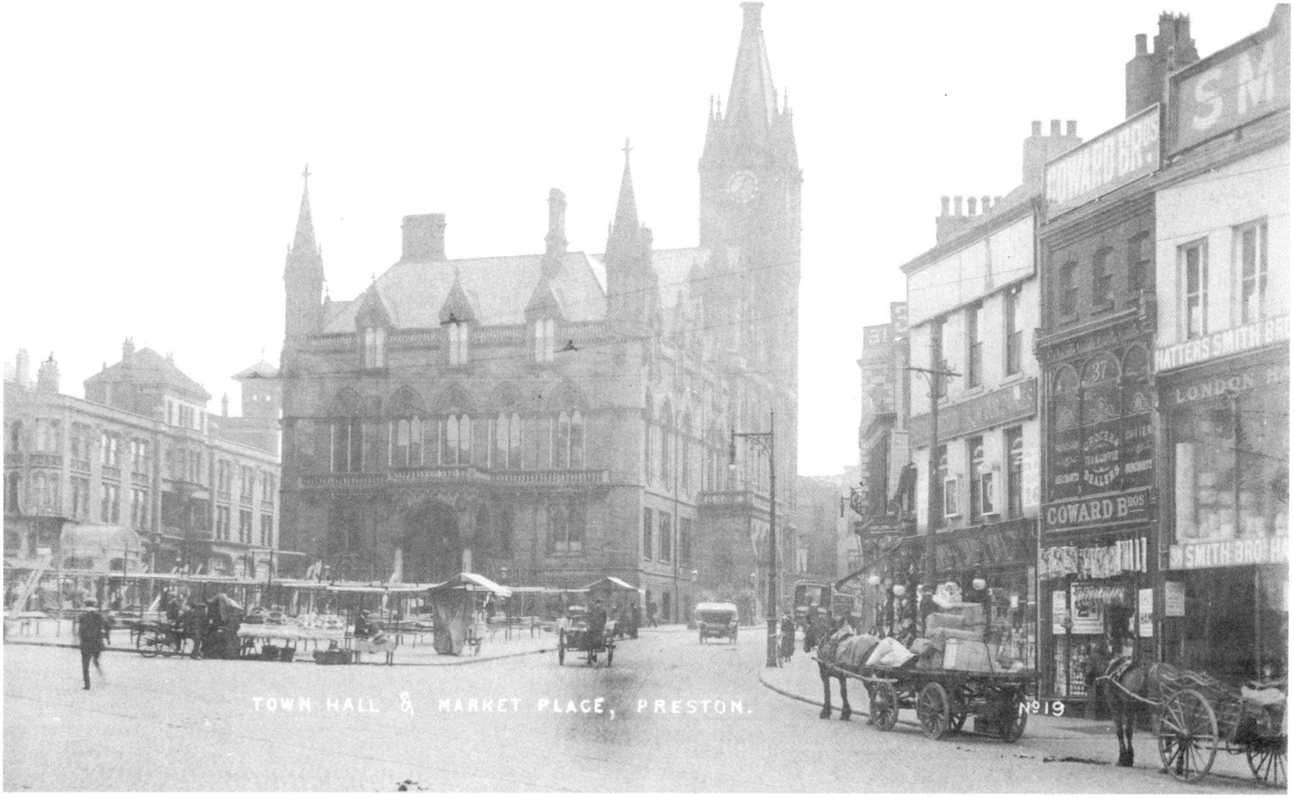

The Market Place with Cheapside and the Town Hall.

'Twenty to one' says the great clock of Preston Town Hall, overlooking an almost deserted Market Place. Only a solitary stall is selling vegetables in the left foreground and there are almost as many horses as there are people in Cheapside, which has been so-called since the early 13th century and derives its name simply from being at the side of the *'Cheap'* or Market. The line of pavement between the two carts on the right leads to Anchor Court, an ancient passageway named after a 17th century hostelry, *The Golden Anchor*, which stood at its Friargate entrance just out of the picture. The elaborate shopfront on the right at No.37 is that of Coward Brothers, grocers, tea and coffee dealers and butter merchants, a long-established company, formerly Coward & Wilding, which had based its *'wonderful success'* on being *'direct importers, saving all intermediate profits, which go into the pockets of their customers, instead of those of middlemen'*. Further to the left, at No. 36 is a company familiar to older locals, the Maypole Dairy Co., which always had a clean, buttery, greaseproof paperish smell when one walked in. The reason for this was that the staff made up each pack of butter, shaping it with ridged butter pats. Many will remember the sound of those butter pats, and see in their mind's eye the ridges made in the butter – it all seemed to make it taste better! When this photograph was taken, the first floor was occupied by a photographer, J. T. Wright. Immediately beyond, barely visible, is the gabled roof of a 17th century half-timbered building, 34 and 35, then occupied by the Misses Barlow, hosiers (now Yates' jewellers) and R. Butler, bootmaker, whose gutter shows just halfway up the front of the Maypole. Beyond these on the roofline can be seen No.31, Stead & Simpson's, boot manufacturers, and Nos. 32 and 33, J. Hamilton & Son, drapers. Interestingly, across Fishergate can be seen (to the left) the premises of Freeman, Hardy & Willis, boot manufacturers, and (to the right) Crompton's pharmacy, pulled down a couple of years later to open up Glover's Court to Fishergate.

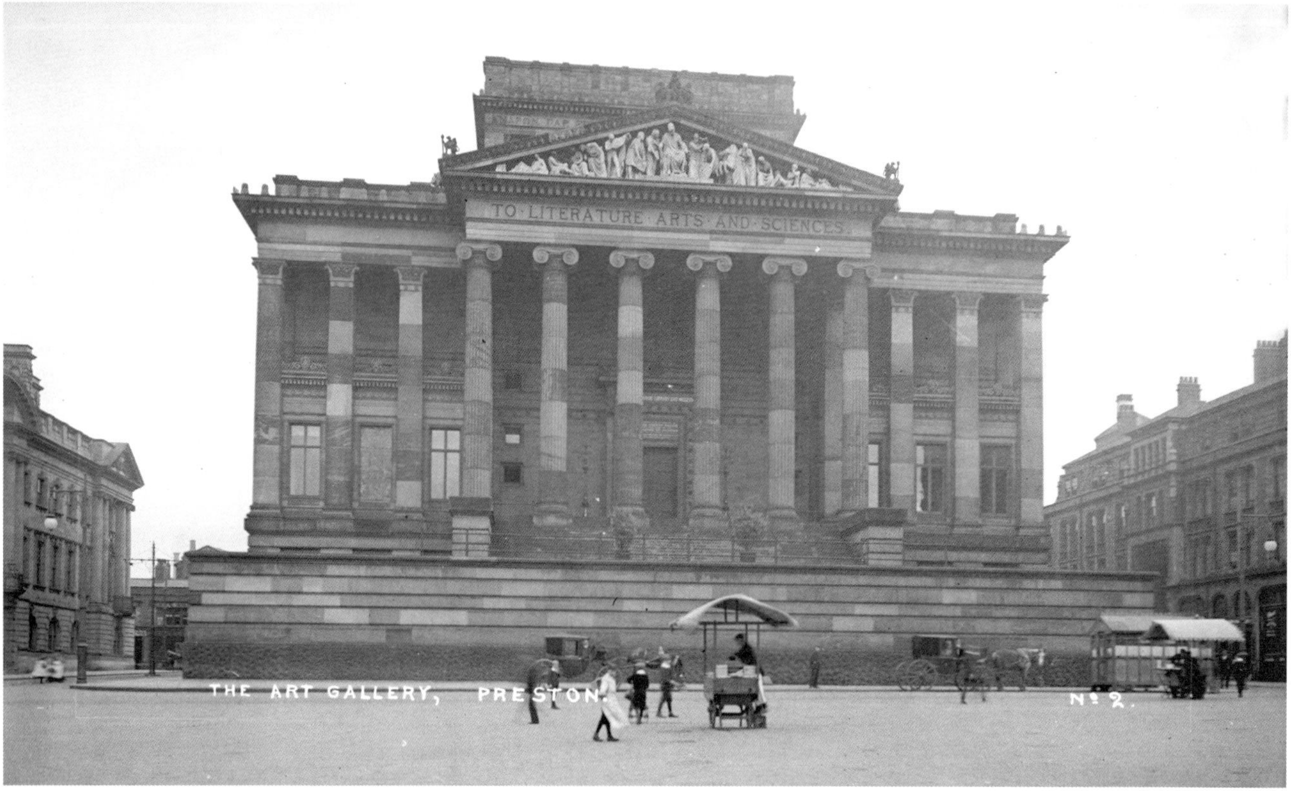

The Harris Library, Museum and Art Gallery.

In 1879, the Trustees of the late Edmund Robert Harris agreed to donate a fortune of £100,000 towards the building of a *'Free Public Library and Museum'*. James Hibbert, a local architect and Alderman of Preston, was selected to prepare the designs. He had already demonstrated his skills in designing the very fine Fishergate Baptist Church in an Italian Romanesque style, and Preston Royal Infirmary, which had been inspired by architecture of the French Renaissance; but for the Harris building he chose the neo-Greek style. In presenting his designs, he declared that *'the intention and meaning of the entire structural design, both externally and internally, may be regarded as an endeavour to uphold, and carry onward the tradition of Hellenic art'*. Hibbert had derived his inspiration not from Greece, but from the Opera House, Berlin, designed by Karl Friedrich Schinkel and built in 1818-21. He looked elsewhere for other features; to the great Rostra in the Roman Forum (used by the rulers of the Empire to address their peoples) for the massive wall fronting the Market Place; to Napoleon's tomb in the Invalides, Paris, for the ring balcony near the Reference Library; and to the Greek Court at the Great Exhibition of 1851 for the balconies and furniture of the central lantern. The Harris Library, Museum and Art Gallery, one of the truly great neoclassical buildings in the United Kingdom, was James Hibbert's brainchild. For 17 years he was professionally involved with it, an association which ultimately became an obsession. He retired and went to live in London in March 1898, taking with him a large volume of the original plans for his Hellenic creation. The volume, now in the Central Reference Library of the Harris building, has a title page which describes him not as *Alderman*, but as *Senator*. In the photo a stallholder is standing on a box to reach over the stall, which has its counterpart in today's jacket potato and parched pea stalls. One of the youngsters queuing at the stall wears a white apron – could he have come out of one of the nearby shops to get a snack?

The Sessions House, Market Place.

Preston Sessions House, or Preston's *'Old Bailey'* as it was popularly called, was opened in 1903. It stood on the site of two ancient streets, Gin Bow Entry, which, as its name implies, led to a corn-mill in medieval times; and Lord Street, where the corn-merchants and their descendants, who used the mill down to the early 19th century, had their warehouses. An east section of Lord Street still survives, running from Lancaster Road to the Central Bus Station along the side of the Guild Hall. The magnificent courthouse, designed by the county architect, Henry Littler, is surmounted by an elegant octagonal tower, which owes much of its inspiration to the baroque architecture of Sir Christopher Wren. The sculpted figures on the façade executed by Gilbert Seale, sculptor at the Old Bailey, are symbolic of the system of British justice: – over the window of the main doorway are figures representing *Justice* with her scales, and *Mercury*, a god of justice in classical mythology. Flanking the base of the tower are two monumental figures of *Hercules*, representing power and authority, and *Britannia* herself. Justice, of course, must be impartial, and the cherubs over the windows of the lower storey are blindfolded. Then, as now, the public entrance was in Lancaster Road, while that for prisoners was on the side facing Market Square. There were eleven cells *'provided for 70 or 75 prisoners awaiting trial'*; there was *'a library, robing-room and smoke-room, beautifully fitted up in Dantzig oak'* for the barristers; and there were also *'excellent rooms'* for the caretaker. In short, everyone was happy! In the Market Place, stalls are laid out with fresh produce, long before the days before it all had to be under cover in the Market Hall. All the stallholders in view appear to be men – no women around at all.

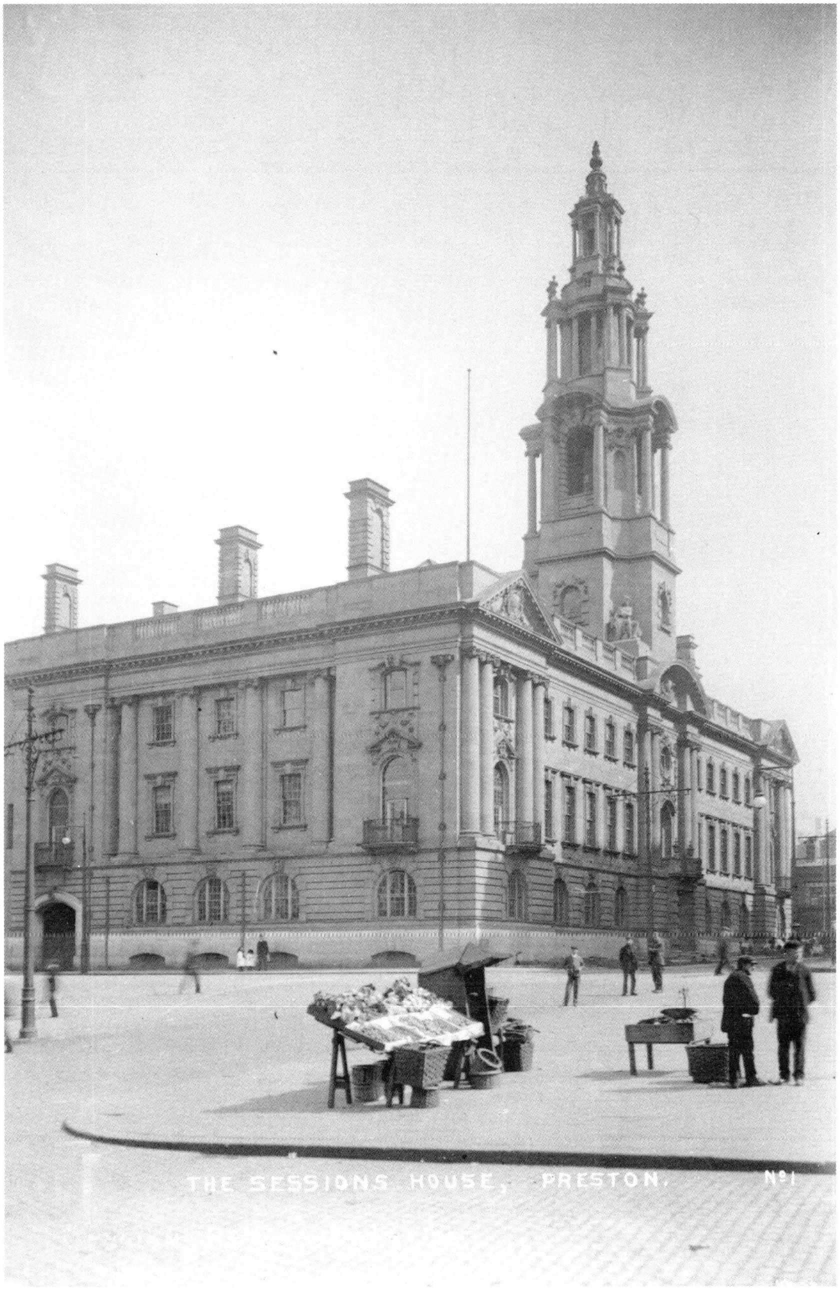

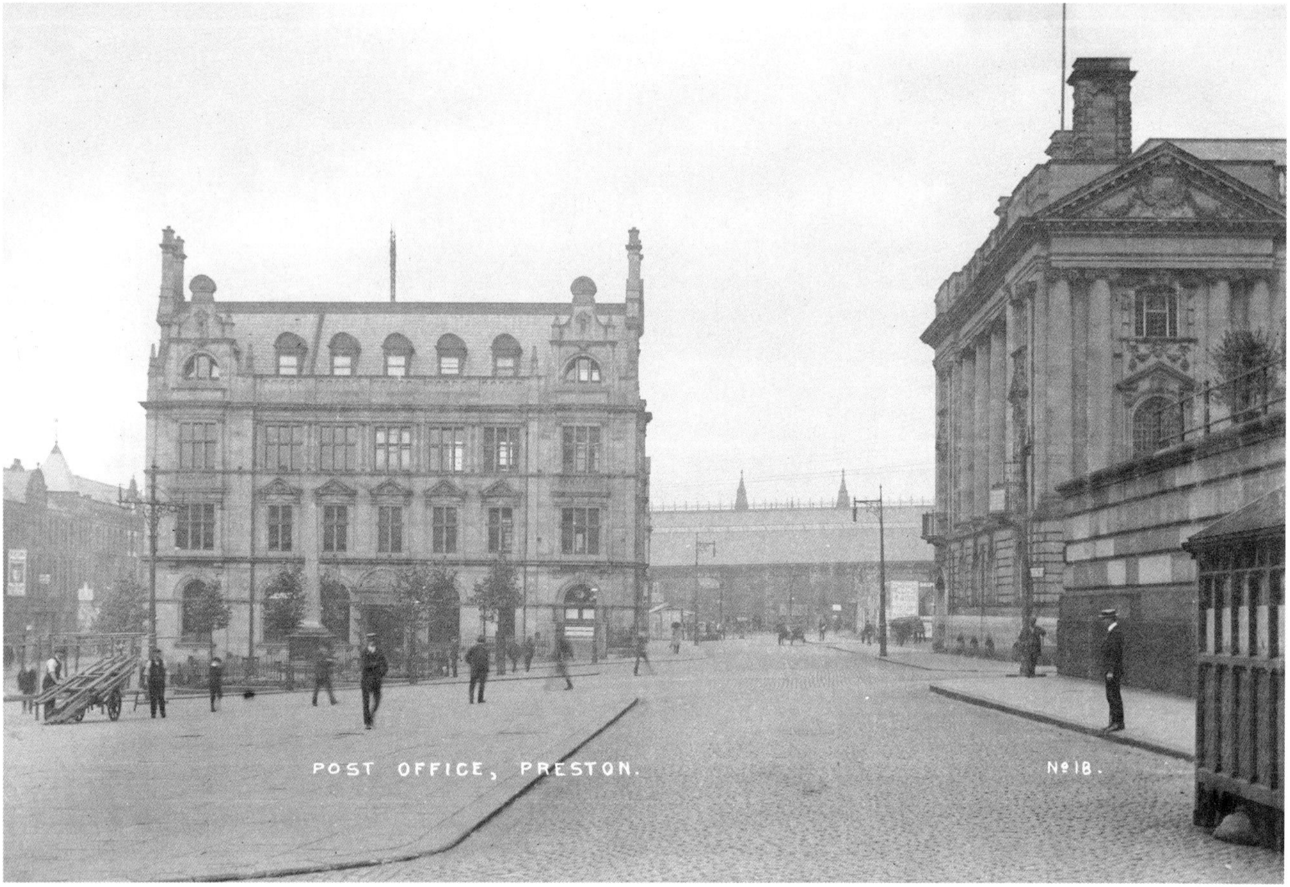

The Central Post Office, Market Place.

When Alderman Edmund Birley, senior member of a cotton-mill owning family and Mayor of the Merchant Guild of 1882, died on March 28, 1895, it was naturally thought that his name should be perpetuated. Shortly afterwards, a new road, shown here on the photograph, which ran from Fishergate, along the front of the Harris building and through to the covered market, was named Birley Street. Just beyond the covered market can be seen the two Gothic spires of the Orchard Methodist Chapel, opened in May 1862 and demolished a century later. On the left is the Central Post Office, designed by Henry Tanner and opened on August 24, 1903. This splendid building, with its elaborate Dutch gables, a popular late 19th century revival of English Jacobean architecture, completed a phase of building round the Market Place which began with the Old Town Hall, 1862-67, the Harris Library and Museum, 1882-91, and the Sessions House, 1901-03. Birley Street in front of the Harris building is now paved over as part of the Market Square, but its ghost is marked out in the lines of the cycle route. There is a noticeable absence in this photograph, – the present Town Hall. The Municipal Building, as it used to be called, only arrived on the scene in 1933. When this photograph was taken, the plot of ground it now occupies was known as *'cinder pad'*, where the local youths played football. Immediately on the right is the cabbies' shelter.

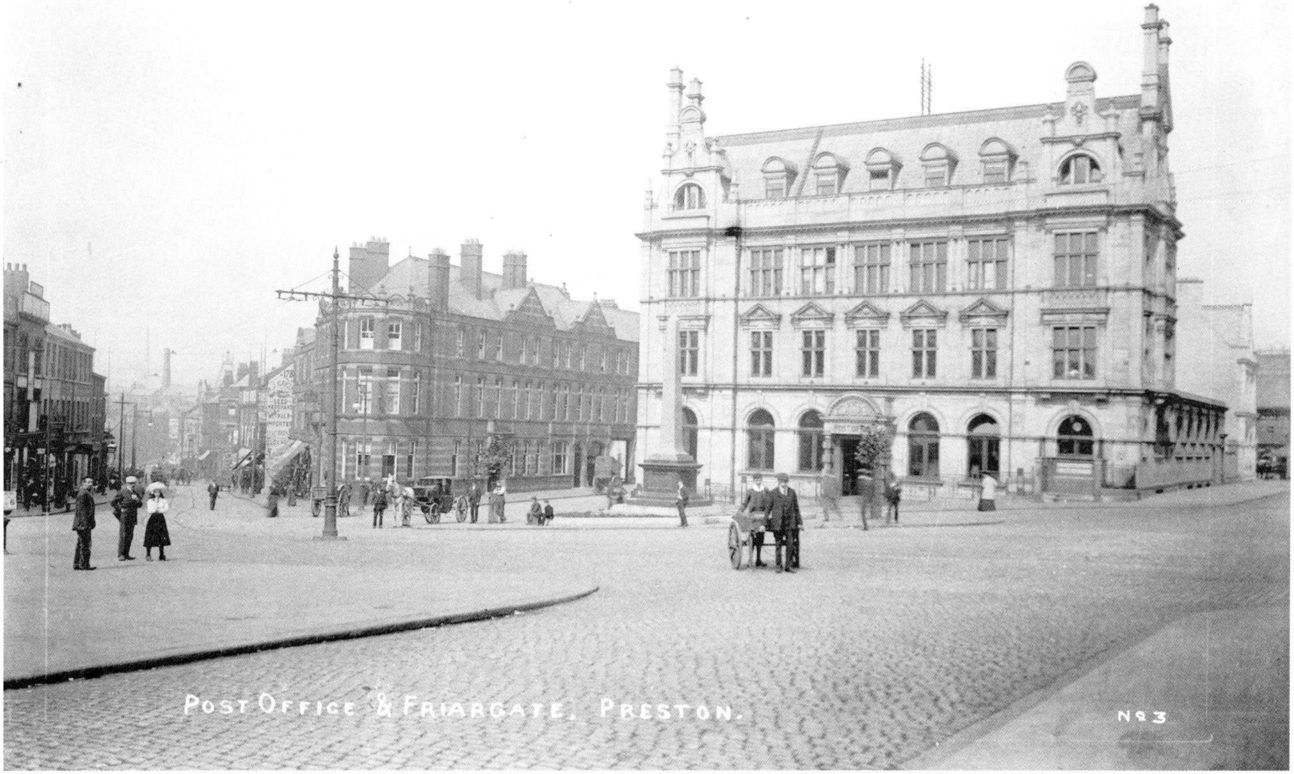

Market Place looking towards Friargate.

In front of the Central Post Office is the Boer War Memorial, ceremonially unveiled on October 6, 1904, but which, following the huge number of casualties in the First World War, was removed to Avenham Park and replaced by the present Cenotaph in 1926. When this photograph was taken, the corner of Friargate and Market Street was occupied by William Bee's *George Inn*, named after a 17th century hostelry, the *Sign of the George*, owned by Edward Craven. Colonel Bellingham, an Officer in the Royalist army, dined there on March 6, 1689, and recorded in his diary: *'came to Ned Craven's where we had stinking oysters'*. The old inn was demolished in 1895 along with the rest of the ramshackle, vermin-infested properties on the north side of Market Place. The new building, designed by Swindells and Rawcliffe of Preston, that was erected on the site, included a 'new' *George Inn* at its Friargate corner. Just visible on the left of the photograph is a drinking fountain, which was removed shortly after this photograph was taken. It was described in 1821 as *'sometimes used for the purposes of a whipping post for offenders guilty of misdemeanours within the borough; handcuffs are fixed to the body of the pump'*. Many people in the photograph appear to be posed; the men with the cart in the foreground; the coach at the corner of Market Street; and the two men and a lady, set against a background of Friargate. Could it be that they are standing still to be part of the photograph?

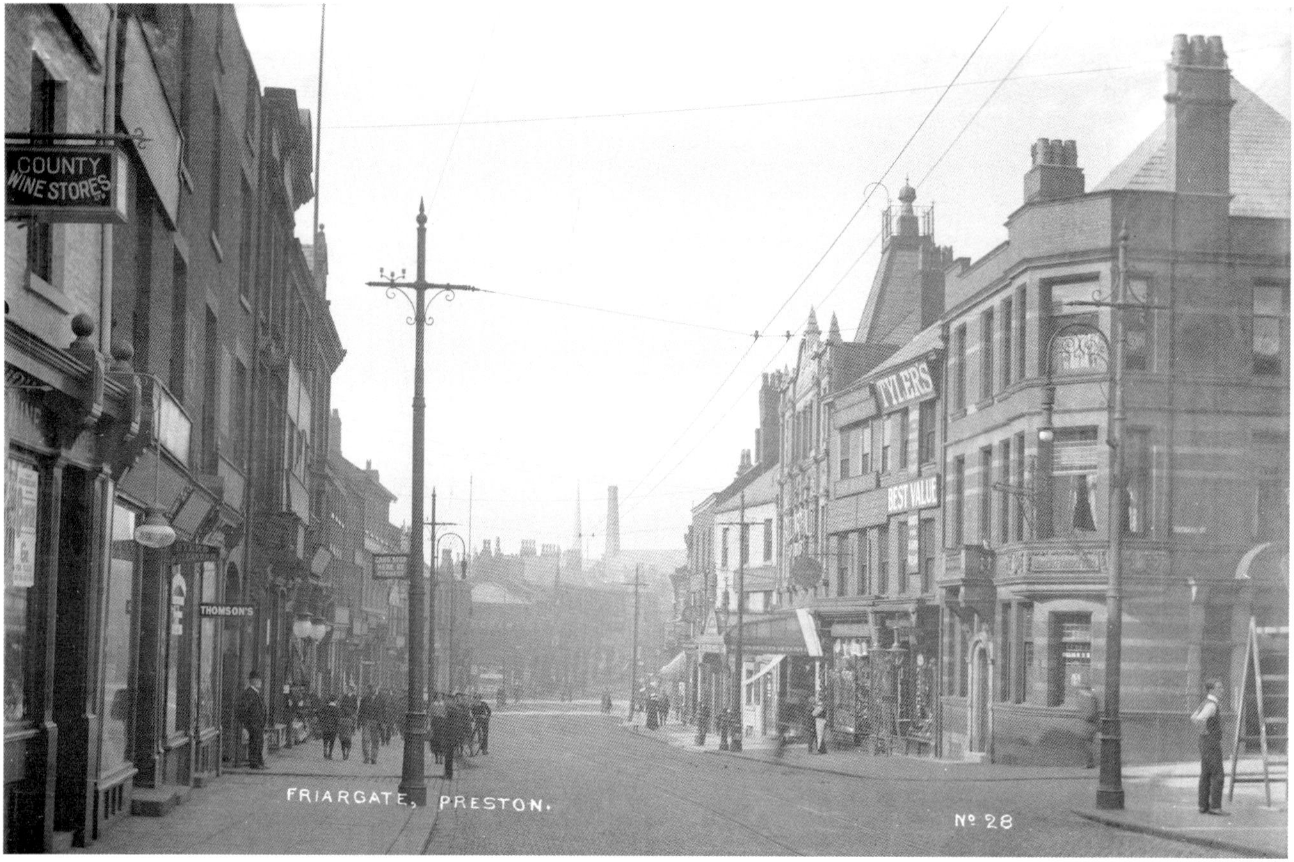

Friargate from the Black Horse, Orchard Street.

From Saxon times to the construction of Lancaster Road in 1827, Friargate was the main route to the north from Market Place. However, its name is derived from being the *'gate'* or *'way'* to the Monastery of the Friars Minor, built in 1221 and situated immediately south west of the junction of Ladywell Street and Marsh Lane. No trace of the monastery survives but the name lives on. By contrast, Orchard Street, shown here on the right, only dates from 1836 when it was constructed to allow easier access to a public space called *'the Orchard'*, now occupied by the covered market. At its corner is the *Black Horse* public house, seen here after a red-brick face-lift in 1898. The splendid interior decoration, particularly the stained glass round the bar, which dates from the same time, is well worth a visit. Beyond it is a notice BEST VALUE on Henry Tyler's boot and shoe shop; and next door, Slinger's, furnishing ironmongers and tool merchants, specialist saw-mill engineers and saw makers. Next to Slinger's is the Hippodrome Theatre, opened on Monday, January 16, 1905, with Charles Coburn, the legendary actor/singer on stage. Although the Hippodrome closed in 1957, pause when you pass this spot, for General Booth, founder of the Salvation Army, preached here on Sunday, November 5th, 1905. Across the road is an archway leading to Bamber's Yard which, when this photograph was taken, was a thriving shopping centre of boot-makers, builders, coopers, cloggers; with plumbers cheek-by-jowl with fancy goods makers, tailors and drapers. It was demolished in 1963 during the construction of St. George's Shopping Centre. A sign on the pylon supporting the tram wires outside Thomson's on the left reads CARS STOP HERE BY REQUEST; that is, of course, tram cars.

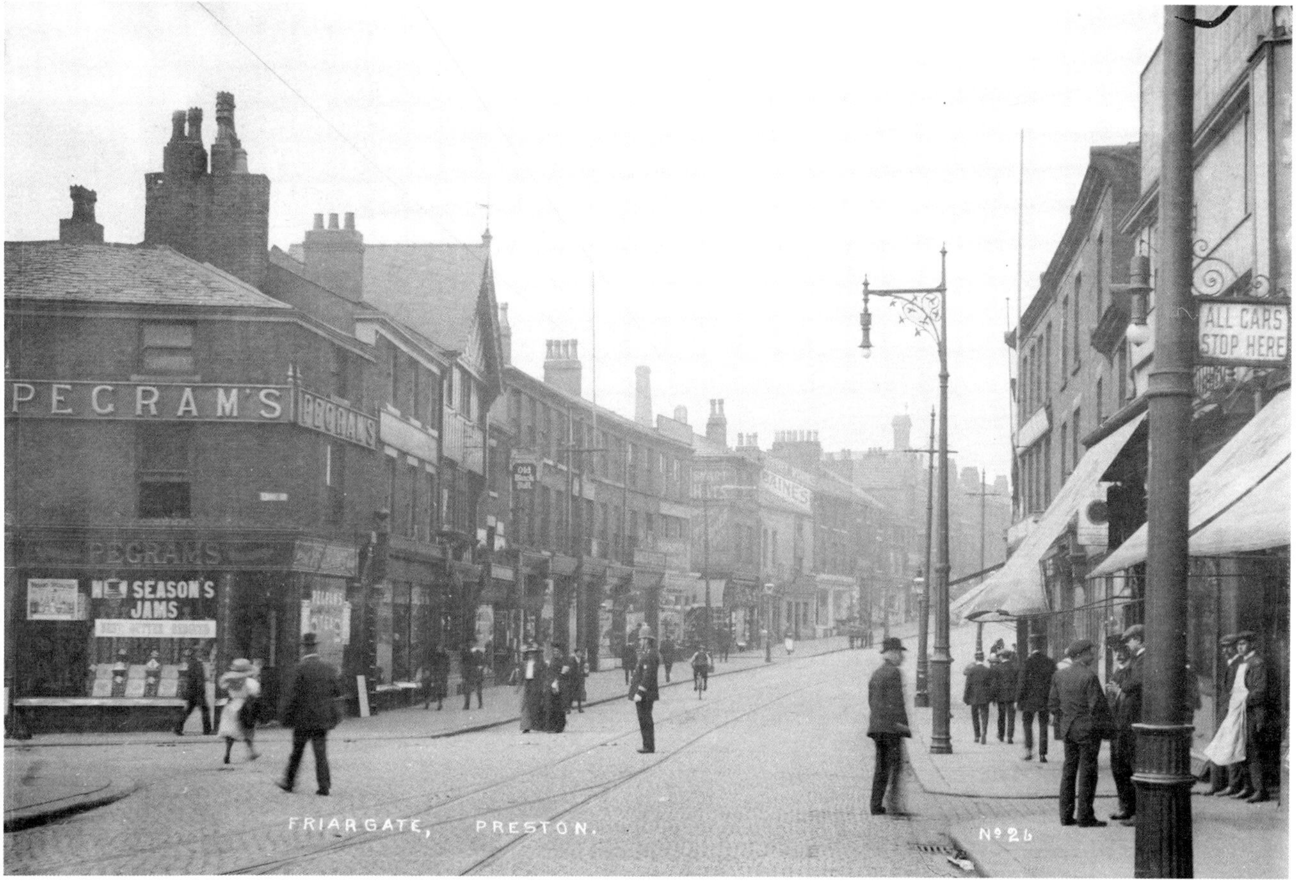

Friargate from Lune Street.

A policeman stares abstractedly whilst a young lady, wearing a hat that is as wide as her shoulders, strides purposefully across the Lune Street entrance to Friargate. Although Friargate is an ancient road, Lune Street was only constructed in 1802 as a road leading to the Lancaster Canal Terminus which many will remember near Corporation Street at the back of the old Public Hall, shown in the next photograph. The more southerly section of Lune Street to Fishergate was only constructed about 1810. Here at the Lune Street corner is the handsome front of James Pegram & Co., tea dealers, advertising their new season's jams. Immediately next door is the double-fronted shop of Hannah Thompson, milliner. The gabled building beyond is the old *Black Bull*, an 18th century hostelry which had acquired an Art Nouveau front of green glazed tiles shortly before this photograph was taken. The other shops beyond the Black Bull are the premises of Yates' confectioners, Edward Worthington, draper, A.M. Crozier, wholesale and retail tobacconists, James Foster, hosier, knitting machine and sewing machine manufacturer, and at the corner of Hill Street, Messrs. Hopkinson and Heaton, house furnishers. On the right, a bowler hatted gentleman hesitates, as if unsure whether to run the gauntlet of two men who, between them, obstruct half of the width of the ginnel on the right. All the properties in the foreground of the picture as far as the *Black Bull* were demolished in the late 1960s to make way for Preston's inner ring-road, Ring Way.

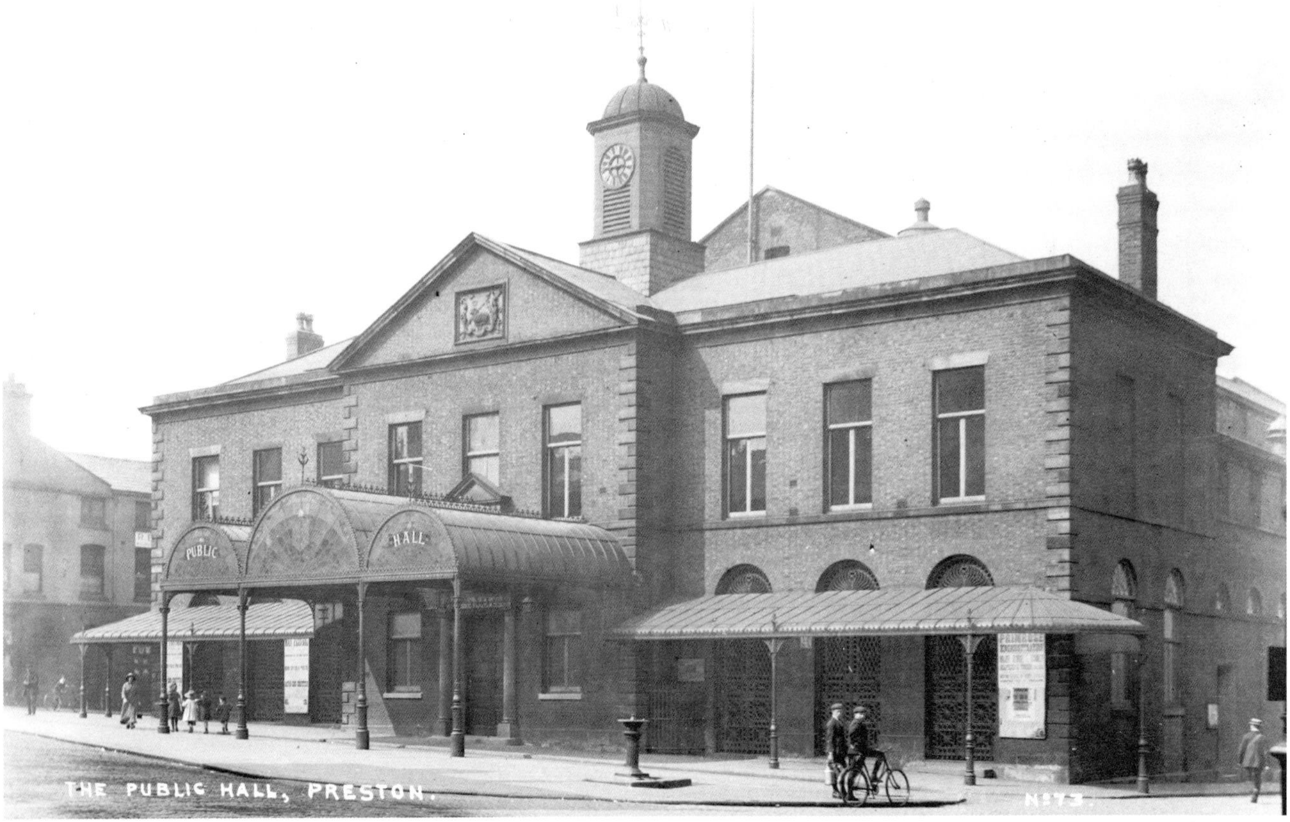

The Old Public Hall.

Preston Public Hall was built in 1824 as a Corn Exchange. It had a Georgian front with clock tower, incorporating Assembly Rooms which were used for public meetings, and rear buildings surrounding an open courtyard. Inspired by a visit to the Great Exhibition, Hyde Park, in 1851, members of Preston Town Council hit on the idea of bridging over the huge area of the courtyard of the Corn Exchange using the same cast iron and glass building technique. The new and improved Corn Exchange opened as the town's first exhibition centre in 1853, and in those early years it was even called *'Preston's Crystal Palace'*! In 1882 the building was radically reconstructed internally for use as a concert hall, to be called *'The Public Hall'*. The exterior walls of the courtyard were demolished to open up the entire width of the building for balconies of seats around the hall. In addition, an elaborate cast iron and glass arcade was set up around the entrance to protect visitors in bad weather. Oddly placed in the triangular pediment over the entrance is the coat of arms of Preston, rescued from the old Preston Town Hall of 1780 when it was demolished in 1862. Among the famous singers, instrumentalists and politicians who have visited the Public Hall, are Franz Liszt, August 27, 1833 (in the old Assembly Rooms); the great soprano, Adelina Patti, in 1890 and 1892; Charles and Lady Halle, in a recital in 1894; Paderewski, the Polish pianist, in 1895; James Kier Hardie, founder of the ILP (Independent Labour Party) in 1901; Asquith in 1904; and in later times all the major politicians of all parties. Now, all that remains of the Public Hall is the Georgian front, converted into a public house, which is called *The Assembly – The Corn Exchange*. To the left, a lady in an overcoat is striding out, oblivious of four children walking along in descending age and size! At the other side of the photograph, a cyclist and his friend, conscious that the camera is pointing towards them, pose to become part of history.

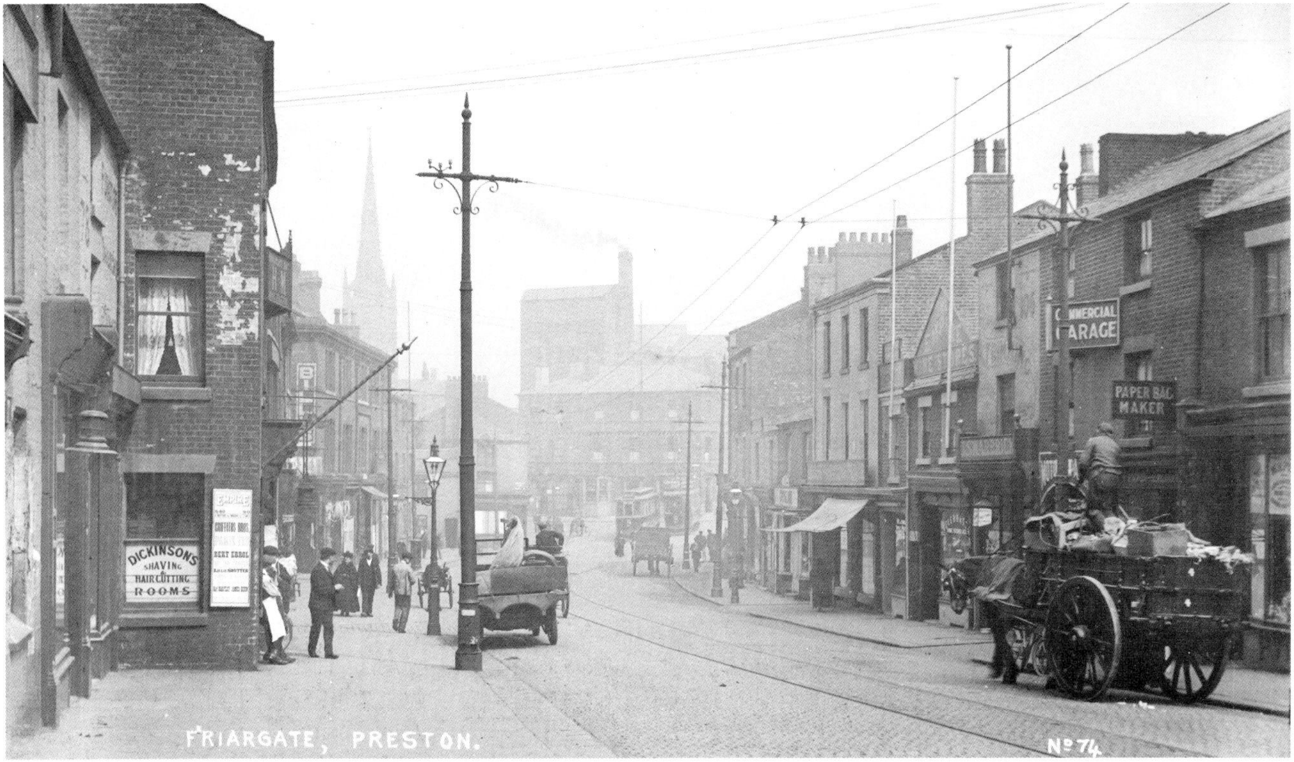

Friargate looking towards the Adelphi Inn.

On the pavement to the left, a man with an apron waits outside Thomas Dickinson's, shaving and hair cutting rooms at 78a, Friargate, who he has permitted, for a consideration, a framed poster for the Empire Theatre in Church Street, advertising the Griffiths Brothers, Bert Errol, and Louise Noufter. On the right, a horse is pulling a loaded cart alongside a line of old properties which include, in the foreground, Michael Tommony's premises at No. 107, over which is a sign *Paper Bag Maker*. Mr. Tommony had been in business as a paper and paper bag manufacturer, and wholesale stationer, since 1873. The shop was a large warehouse which had changed little since 1889, when it was described as *'stocked with paper of every description, including cap papers, brown papers, butter papers, sugar papers, tobacco, tea and coffee papers, printing paper, tissue, demy, jewellers' tissue and mill papers'*. He also had *'a great variety of ledgers, day, cash, and memorandum-books, window tickets, including tin tickets, as writers of which the house has long been famous'*. The lines of the pavement there lead to Tommony's Yard, where a garage for the new motor vehicles has just been set up. It will have joined James Worden, who was already established there as a music and musical instrument dealer. Just round the corner on the right is Walker Street, which must be an alternative route chosen instead of a street mentioned in an article in *The Preston Chronicle* of February 27, 1836, *'to be called Moor Park Street, which will run from the back of the Fighting Cocks in a direct line North East to a little beyond the Windmill in Moor Lane – cutting off a crooked portion of that lane on the South and forming in place of it a wider and more direct entrance to the Lancaster Road into Friargate'*. Facing us across the end of Friargate is the *Adelphi* public house, which took over the licence of the *Fighting Cocks Inn* when it was demolished in the 1830s, and is still with us. Beyond the *Adelphi Inn* is Henry Shutt's Green Bank Mill, a corn mill that stood on the site of an 18th century windmill, identical to the last surviving windmill in Cragg's Row, off Moor Lane.

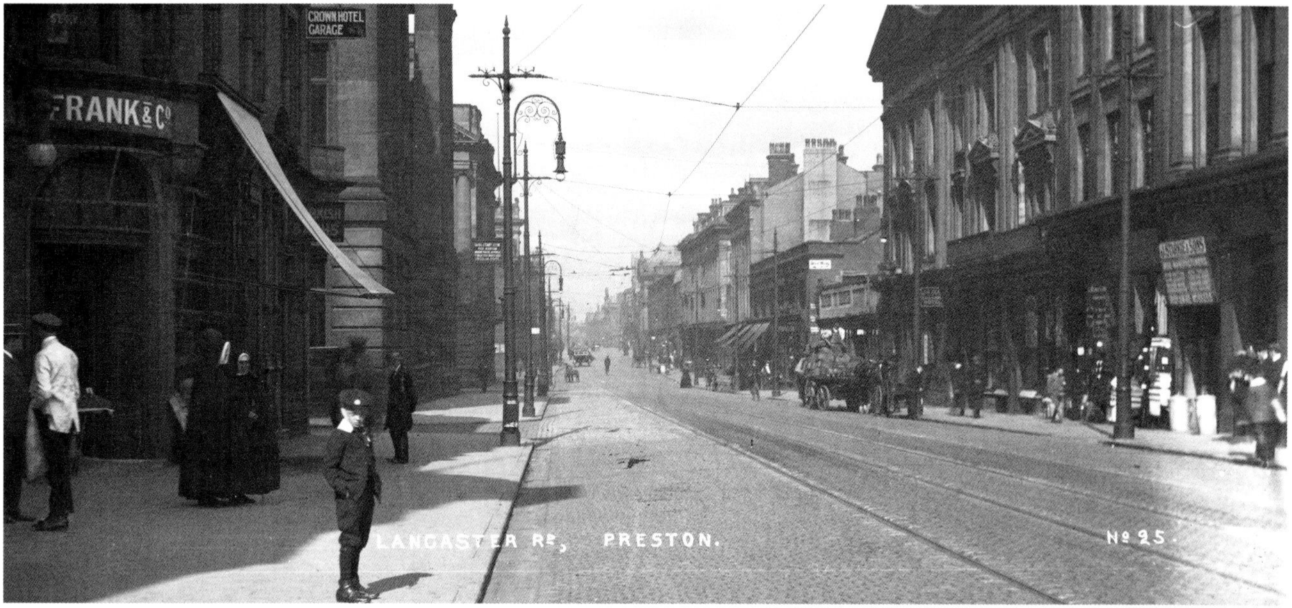

Lancaster Road looking North.

Two nuns pause at the entrance to the Miller Arcade in Lancaster Road. There is certainly temptation behind them, through the doorway of Frank & Co., the high-class fish, fruit, game and poultry dealers, whose only rivals were Heaney's in Fishergate. Immediately over the shop are the premises of Preston Provident Dental Services. Further along is a sign TURKISH BATHS; the sign has gone, but the same words are moulded in the tiles over the doorway to this day. More revealing is the notice above it, CROWN HOTEL GARAGE, advertising that the *Crown Hotel*, at the Market Square corner of the Miller Arcade had all the facilities to cater for those who owned the status symbol of the age, the motor car. The garage sign has gone; the *Crown Hotel* has gone; only the mosaic with the legend CROWN HOTEL survives in the doorway pointing towards Market Square. In 1849, the buildings at the Church Street end of Lancaster Road were demolished, allowing it to become a main route to the north. This opened up the road for development, and Stanley Buildings, on the right of the photograph, was completed in 1854. Its first occupant was the *Stanley Arms*, at the far end, which took its name from the old *Stanley Arms*, one of the buildings destroyed in the road widening scheme. A new Post Office was also opened at the near end on the edge of the photograph. Its predecessor occupied a dingy room in the Old Shambles, which stood almost exactly where the photographer has set up his camera. This earlier Post Office was in use from the 1720s right up to when the new one opened. One of its postmasters, Josiah Johnson, used to tell how on one occasion, in 1835, a letter arrived from Ireland simply addressed to *'No. 5, Preston, England'*. With a flash of intuition, Johnson went to the Penwortham side of the Ribble, where a gang of Irish navvies was constructing the railway embankment leading to the North Union Railway Bridge. *"Is there anyone here called No. 5?"* he shouted. *"Och sure an' that's me"*, said one of them. Johnson asked *"Are you expecting a letter?"* The Irishman replied that his wife in Coleraine was expecting a baby and had promised to get a priest to write to him for her when it arrived. When this photograph was taken, the occupiers of Stanley Buildings were the *Stanley Arms*, with the name, then as now, just below the roofline, the County Drug Store, Hubberstey's grocers, Preston Camera Club, Pearl Life Assurance, Preston and Cottam Hall Brick and Tile Company, and James Starkie & Sons, manufacturers of wire cloth, iron fencing, etc., whose factory was the Wire Works in Cotton Court, Church Street. We see two modes of transport – a heavily laden wagon pulled by a horse, and a handcart pulled by a man. Such transport could have been seen anytime in the last several hundred years; but with the advent of the petrol engine, great changes were afoot.

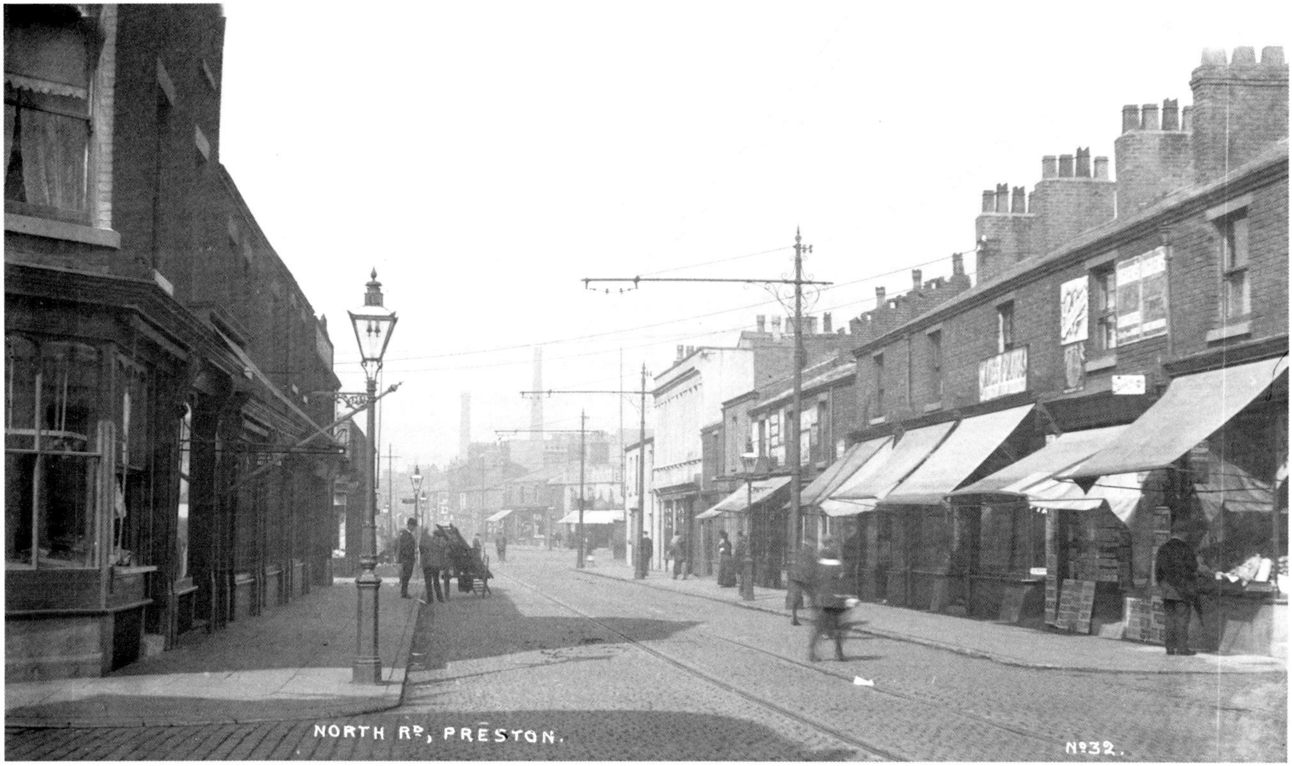

North Road looking North.

North Road was constructed in 1830 to allow for the increased number of coaches heading north from the town centre. All the buildings shown here were swept away in the town improvement schemes of the 1960s, but when this photograph was taken, they were part of a thriving shopping district where you could buy all your daily needs. To give you an idea of where you are looking, – the first shop on the right, Livesey's fruiterers at No. 116, is next door to the *Three Tuns* public house, just out of the picture. Next door we see a newsagent's, run at that time by Miss Margaret Hesketh. At that time, another newsagent's run by a Samuel Hesketh, stood at the corner of Bluebell Yard in Church Street. The Heskeths prospered, and in 1934 were in *'Hesketh's Buildings'* at the top of High Street, seen here on the left, at the corner just out of the picture. The building, with the date carved in stone on the roofline, is still to be seen at the Ormskirk Road corner of Tithebarn Street. Further to the left of Hesketh's is the shop of Joseph Taylor, pianoforte dealer; and then Wood and Eastham, florists; followed by Robert Whalley, confectioner. At the far end of the row is the *Craven Heifer* public house, which marked up a red-letter day on June 3, 1828, when George Green, the celebrated hot air balloonist, and a local joiner called Pemberton, ascended from its back garden. Beyond this, Park Road enters North Road from the right; and further away, over the rooftops, are the shadowy forms of the Great Hanover Street and Primrose Hill mills. In the left foreground is High Street, so called because it led directly to the *Three Tuns* public house, which was the highest point in Preston. Three doors away, at No. 131, is the barber's pole of Jonathan Holden, hairdresser. Hairdressing was very much in demand in those days; there were as many as 107 barber's shops in Preston, including another four in North Road alone. The shops further away from Holden's were occupied by a broker, clogger, draper, and, at the corner of Saul Street, Margaret Eastham's grocer's shop. A straggle of pedestrians walk the pavements, but what really makes the photograph is the gentleman in conversation with a window cleaner at his cart.

St. Jude's Church, St. George's Road.

St. Jude's Church, which stood at the corner of St. Paul's Road and St. George's Road, was consecrated by the Bishop of Manchester on October 19, 1894. Because of the limitations of the site in this heavily built-up area, the church was on a north-south axis; the main entrance porch, shown in the photograph, was at the north west corner of the building. It was designed in the Decorated Gothic style by Bolton architect R. K. Freeman and was built by the Preston contractors Thomas Croft & Sons at a cost of £7,000. When this photograph was taken, a handsome pulpit desk had recently been presented to the church; *'a good vicarage house'* had been erected at a cost of £2,000; and the Rev. A. F. Gaskell had every reason to think that the future of his church was secure. And so it was until July 2002, when demolition contractors reduced it to rubble.

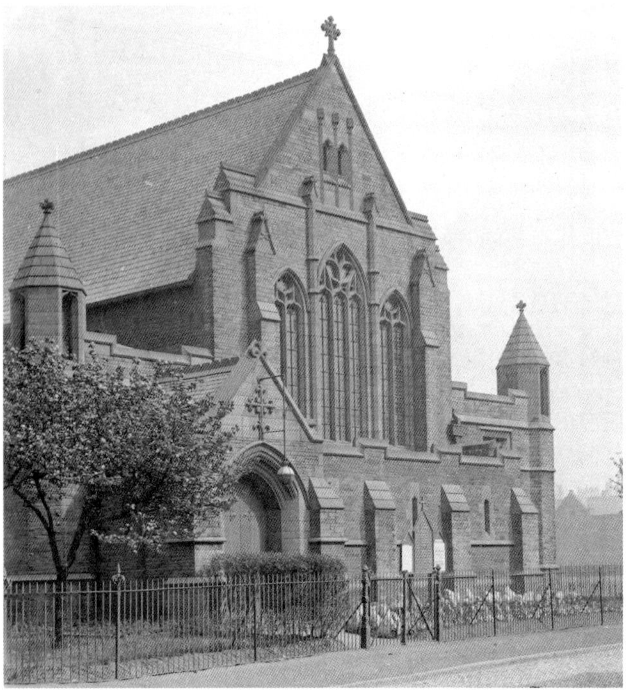

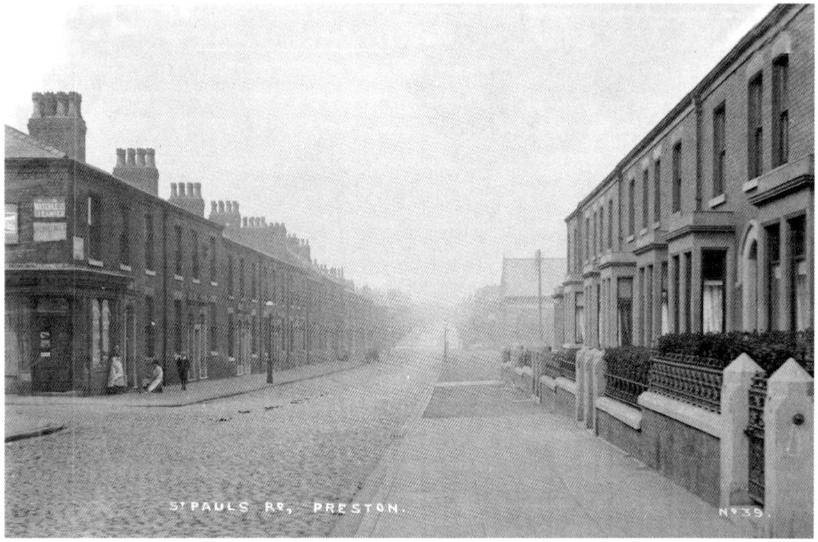

St. Paul's Road looking to Moor Park.

On the left a woman pauses as she scrubs her front doorstep with a donkey-stone. A woman and child with her smile at the cameraman across a cobbled St. Paul's Road. For a century up to 1782 the number of people living in Preston had remained at not more than 6,000. However, the Industrial Revolution brought about a quantum leap in the population as agricultural workers and their families converged on the town to seek employment. In 1801 the population had increased to 11,887; by 1821 it had doubled to 24,627; by 1851 it had trebled on the previous figure to 68,537. To keep up with the increase in numbers, vast areas of the town centre were earmarked for housing development, including the district between Meadow Street and Moor Park. Although the southern part of St. Paul's Road has been developed in recent times, this northern section still survives and retains the old charm it had in this picture. At that time the population of Preston had risen to 118,519. St. Paul's Road and Kent Street follow the line of the principal western Roman Road which passed through the town from the river at Walton, across Church Street near the *Bluebell Inn*, past St. Ignatius' Church (built on Causeway Meadow), continuing approximately between Kent Street and St. Paul's Road, crossing Moor Park near its entrance at the end of this road, and continuing on past Serpentine Lake to Plum Pudding Hill. No trace of this paved road can now be seen, it having been used as a convenient quarry for building stones in the 17th and 18th centuries.

Moor Park Gates, Garstang Road.

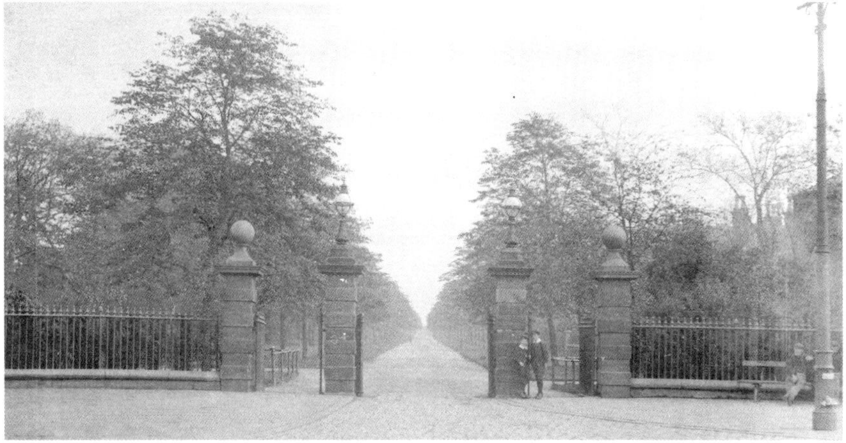

Moor Park, Preston is an historic park of national significance, which may legitimately claim to be the oldest municipal public park in the country. The park as we know it dates from September 28, 1833 when legal steps were taken to abrogate the ancient right of freemen to have pasturage there. Plans were produced which included Moor Park Avenue (then called *Ladies' Walk*) and three lodges designed by the local architect/stonemason John Welch. The original contract stated that the walk *'will be a perfectly straight line of very nearly a mile in length, and it is purposed to have it twenty five yards wide, within fences … The space within these fences will be occupied by a carriage drive in the centre, and grass borders on each side, planted with forest trees, and other shrubs, which, in process of time, will form a grove magnificent in itself'*. In addition, there was to be an ornamental lake and a road, *Serpentine Road*, running along the northern boundary of the park. In the 1860s Edward Milner, chief designer to Joseph Paxton, and one of the outstanding landscape gardeners of his time, was employed to improve the park. He sensitively retained all the features of the original plan; additional roads were made across and round the park; a rockery was constructed at the north west corner; the lake was widened and a footbridge built over it. Apart from the bridge, which sadly was removed several years ago, all the topographical features of Moor Park introduced by Milner survive to the present day. Here we see the entrance gates to Moor Park, showing the *'perfectly straight line'* of *'Ladies' Walk'* as envisaged in the early plans.

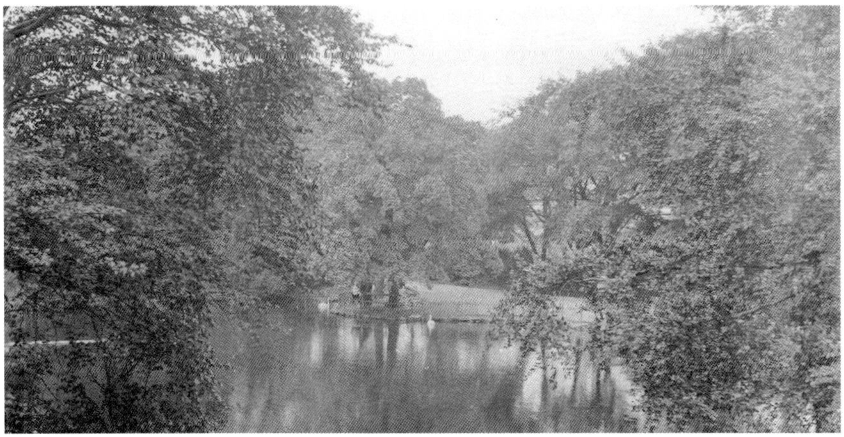

Serpentine Lake, Moor Park.

This photograph illustrates the picturesque Serpentine Lake. Contrasting with the undulating landscape of the lake is a huge flat area of Moor Park to the south and east. This was not a natural feature of the landscape, but specifically designed by Milner to allow for 8,000 troops to be reviewed, or 20,000 to take part in a march past. This was important in Preston, a 19th century garrison town which had a history of civil unrest. Immediately to the north of the lake when this photograph was taken was Serpentine Road, the northern boundary of the park. Serpentine Road became part of Blackpool Road, constructed in the later 1920s and early 1930s. By a strange coincidence, just as the later additions to Moor Park were accomplished by out-of-work cotton operatives during the *Cotton Famine* of the 1860s, so Blackpool Road was constructed by unemployed workers during the *Depression*.

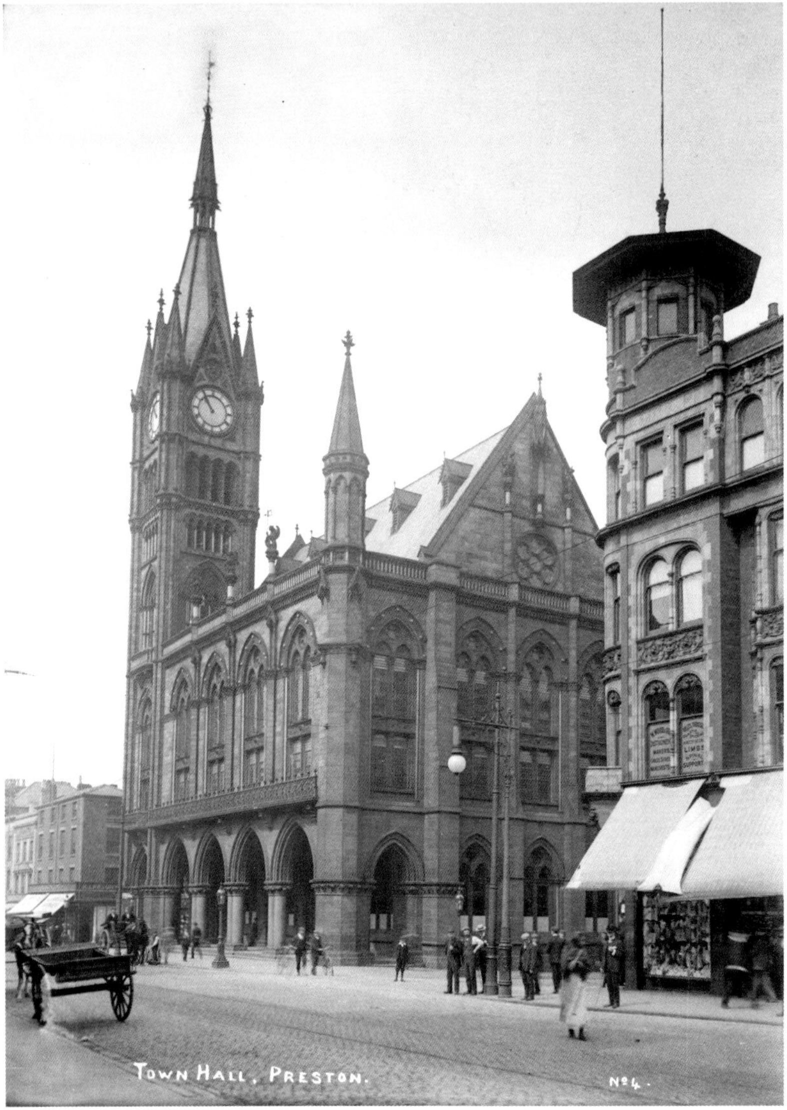

The Old Town Hall.

A young woman, lost in thought and wearing a shawl and clogs, walks aimlessly in the middle of the road, unaware that she is going to be part of one of the finest photographs ever taken of Preston's Old Town Hall, which stood between Market Square and Fishergate. Built during the privations of the *Cotton Famine* in the 1860s, and designed by Sir George Gilbert Scott, it was the admiration of all who saw it until the disastrous fire of March 15th *(The Ides of March),* 1947. Visitors to Ypres in Belgium will know the great Cloth Hall there; built in medieval times, blown to pieces in the First World War, and lovingly rebuilt in the following years. That building is the direct source of Scott's inspiration which gave to Preston what is almost universally recognised as having been one of the most beautiful town halls to have been erected in Great Britain. Its only blemish, as was very correctly pointed out at the time, that the wonderful clock tower and fine arcade of pink polished columns of Aberdonian granite were facing the wrong way!!! As the principal façade, it should have opened up on to the Market Place, as at Ypres, rather than fronting Fishergate, where the comparative narrowness of the road in relation to its height and width prevented one getting sufficiently far enough away to appreciate it. The position chosen by the Shaws for their photograph speaks for itself. The Miller Arcade, to its right, still survives as an important listed building of its age. Here it is before the large corner turrets with their extraordinary projecting eaves were removed for reasons of safety. The corner shop is that of John Dawson, hosier and glover, of No. 1 Miller Arcade. We can all admire the Town Hall in this photograph; but it is brought to life by the glimpse of ordinary everyday life in Fishergate.

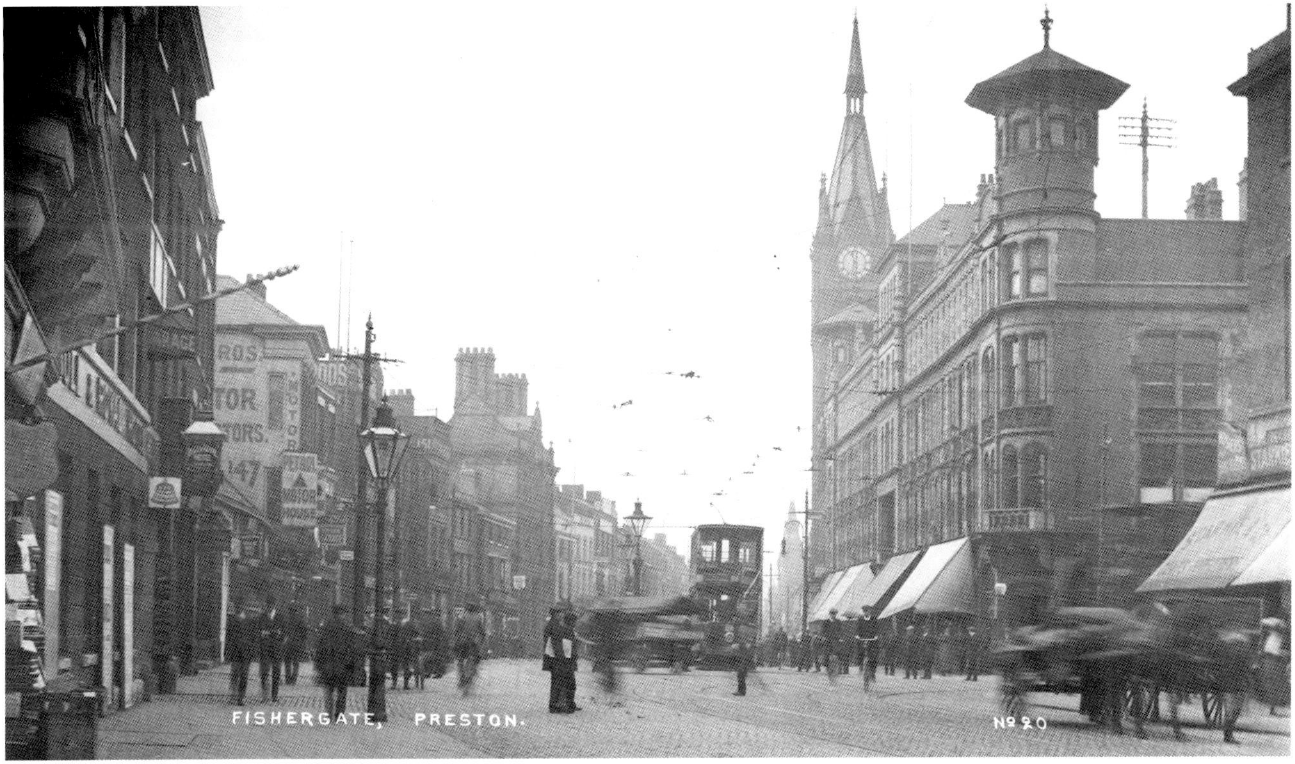

Church Street with the Miller Arcade.

Half past eleven, and the photographer has set up his camera near the Conservative Working Men's Club. On the near left is the barber's pole of William Henry Smith, hairdresser and tobacconist of 80a Church Street. The premises had been a barber's shop for some 180 years when this picture was taken. Next door one can see trays of books belonging to the Discount Book Company. Then we come to the *Bull & Royal Hotel*, known by the sign of the *White Bull* in the 17th century, and which gained its present name when it amalgamated with a *Royal Hotel* next door. During the Battle of Preston in 1715, it was the hospital of the Jacobite Rebels. Robert Patten, chaplain to General Forster, leader of the Rebels, describes how a Peter Farquharson of Rochaley, *'being shot through the Bone of his Leg, endured a great deal of Torture in the Operation of the Surgeon. When he was first brought into the Inn call'd the White Bull, the House where all the wounded Men were carry'd to be dress'd, he took a Glass of Brandy, and said, Come, Lads, here is our Master's Health; tho' I can do no more, I wish you good success. His Leg was cut off by an unskilful Butcher, rather than a Surgeon, and he presently died'.* A new sign of the times is an advertisement on the wall beyond *Yates' Wine Lodge*, PETROL – MOTOR HOUSE, belonging to Merigold Brothers, cycle and motor factors and repairers, and athletic outfitters, at No. 147. The tall building at the west corner of Avenham Road (seen just touching the lamp of the gaslight in the foreground of the photograph) belonged to W. H. & J. Woods, tobacco and cigarette manufacturers, wholesale tobacco and cigar merchants, and dealers in tobacconists' fancy goods, whose name printed on the brickwork survives to this day. On the right is the Miller Arcade, constructed in the last years of the 1890s as Preston's equivalent of Harrods in London. Its Lancaster Road corner was occupied by the *King's Arms Hotel*, with its Long Vault and Wine Stores, whose proprietor at the time was John Hayhurst. The *King's Arms* took its name and licence from the old *King's Arms*, a 17th century hostelry which had stood nearby until it was demolished to make way for the Miller Arcade.

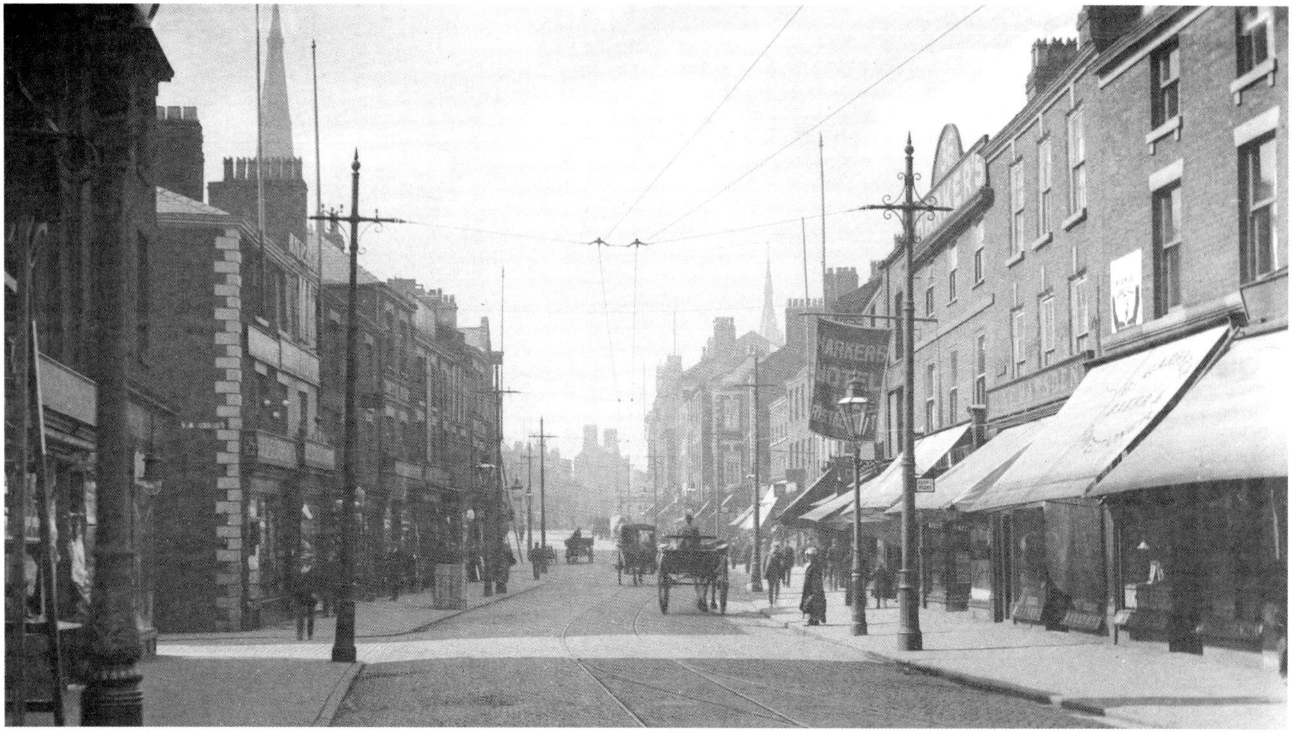

Church Street near Manchester Road.

Horse-drawn vehicles, silhouetted against a sunny Church Street, conjure up a wistful recollection of things past. The road on the left has only been called *Manchester Road* since the turn of the century; before that it was called *Water Street*; and long, long before that, in the 17th century, it was called *Cocker Hole Lane*. However, even though it has a new name, it could make a claim to be the oldest road in Preston. It follows the line of the ditch on the western side of the principal Roman Road to the north, which crossed the road near this spot, and may well have become established as a road in Saxon times when its predecessor fell into disrepair and was used as a quarry for building stones. The shop on its further corner, No. 125, is that of William Hayhurst, pawnbroker, marked by the three balls hanging outside the premises. There were 21 pawnbrokers in Preston when this photograph was taken, but Hayhurst's was the only one in Church Street, or for that matter, in Fishergate and Friargate. Next door at No. 126, are the premises of Richard Myerscough, Ltd., *'wholesale provision merchants, importers of Irish, Danish and French butter, and sole manufacturers of M.P. Royal Patent sausages'*. The M.P. sausages were described as *'not only noted for uniform wholesomeness and reliability, but also for their exceptional digestive and nutritive qualities – qualities secured by an improved method of preparation, invented by the proprietor'*. A line across the pavement beyond, marks the entrance to the yard of the *Old Dog Inn*. It is an ancient inn with a history that stretches back to the 17th century. However, strange as it may seem, it is remembered as having been the birthplace of Methodism in Preston. In 1776, its landlady, Mrs. Walmsley, became friendly with the first Preston Methodist, Martha Thompson, who attended meetings, not in Preston but in Brimicroft, six miles away. Mrs. Walmsley and her son, William, were converted to the new faith and allowed the Methodists to use one of the rooms at the *Old Dog* for their services. On the right, a large banner marks out Mrs. Harker's Commercial Hotel and Restaurant, at No. 36. The Harker family also owned Harker's Empress Café at No. 29a. Not one piece of litter is to be found in the road or on the pavements!

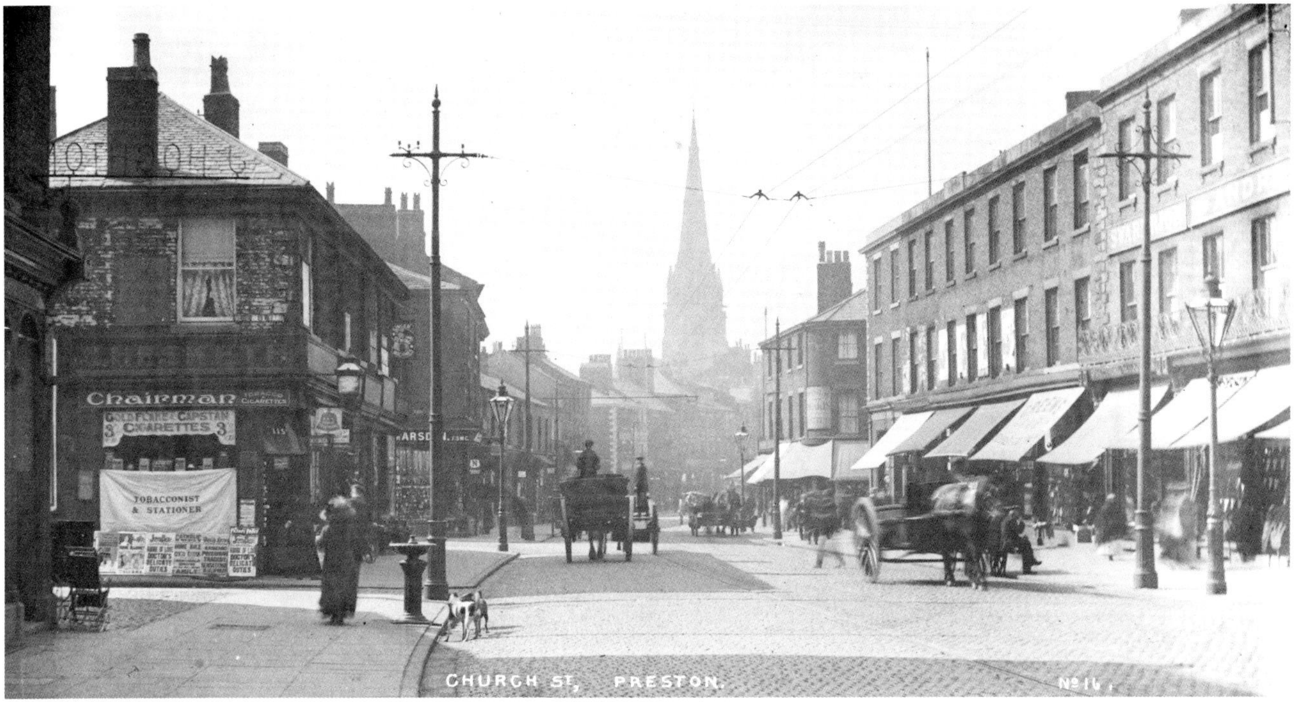

Church Street from near the Blue Bell Inn.

A lady pauses near the old fountain in Church Street. She has just seen a Daily News billboard ARSENIC POISONING TRAGEDY: SENSATIONAL DEVELOPMENT at Hesketh's newsagents. When one thinks of arsenic, one thinks of Frederick Seddon, whose sensational trial and the run up to it, for the murder of Eliza Mary Barrow held the public spellbound in1911 and early 1912. Miss Barrow was a rich lodger of Seddon and his wife, who lived in north London. With her permission he began to manage her financial affairs; but suddenly she fell violently ill and died ten days later. Her relations became suspicious, because no application had been made to bury her in the family vault at Highgate Cemetery and Seddon had been named as her executor. Police exhumed the body, which was found to contain a fatal dose of arsenic. At his trial, it was revealed that fly-papers, then coated with arsenic, had been hung around Miss Barrow's bed, presumably to kill disease ridden flies. Although there was no evidence that arsenic had specifically been administered to her, Seddon was found guilty and hanged. The trial has also gone down in history because the day after it finished, newspapers showed a photograph of Seddon being sentenced to death. When this photograph was taken, you could have bought ten Gold Flake or Capstan cigarettes in Hesketh's for threepence; five Woodbines would have cost you a penny. To the left is Blue Bell Yard and, just out of view, the old *Blue Bell Inn*, its presence only marked by some cobbles on the pavement, which are there to this day. This old inn has been serving ale since at the very least April 30, 1716, when a *'Widow Hall of the Blew Ball'* was fined £2 for keeping a disorderly house there (!) Just visible against Hesketh's roof are the reversed wrought-iron letters of a sign belonging to John Hoghton, pram maker (and there is a pram just outside his shop). Beyond Hesketh's, at the corner of Grimshaw Street, can be seen the shop of Richard Marsden, optician, photographic dealer and tool merchant. On the right is a large building, the predecessor of the present one, which stood on the site of a mansion, Patten House, and which belonged to the family of the Earls of Derby – this was demolished in 1835. At the far end of the building is Thomas Blogg's York Hotel at No. 46, which stood at the corner of the aptly named Derby Street. But above all else in this splendid photograph is the fascinating hustling and bustling scene with carters standing in their wagons as they drive along.

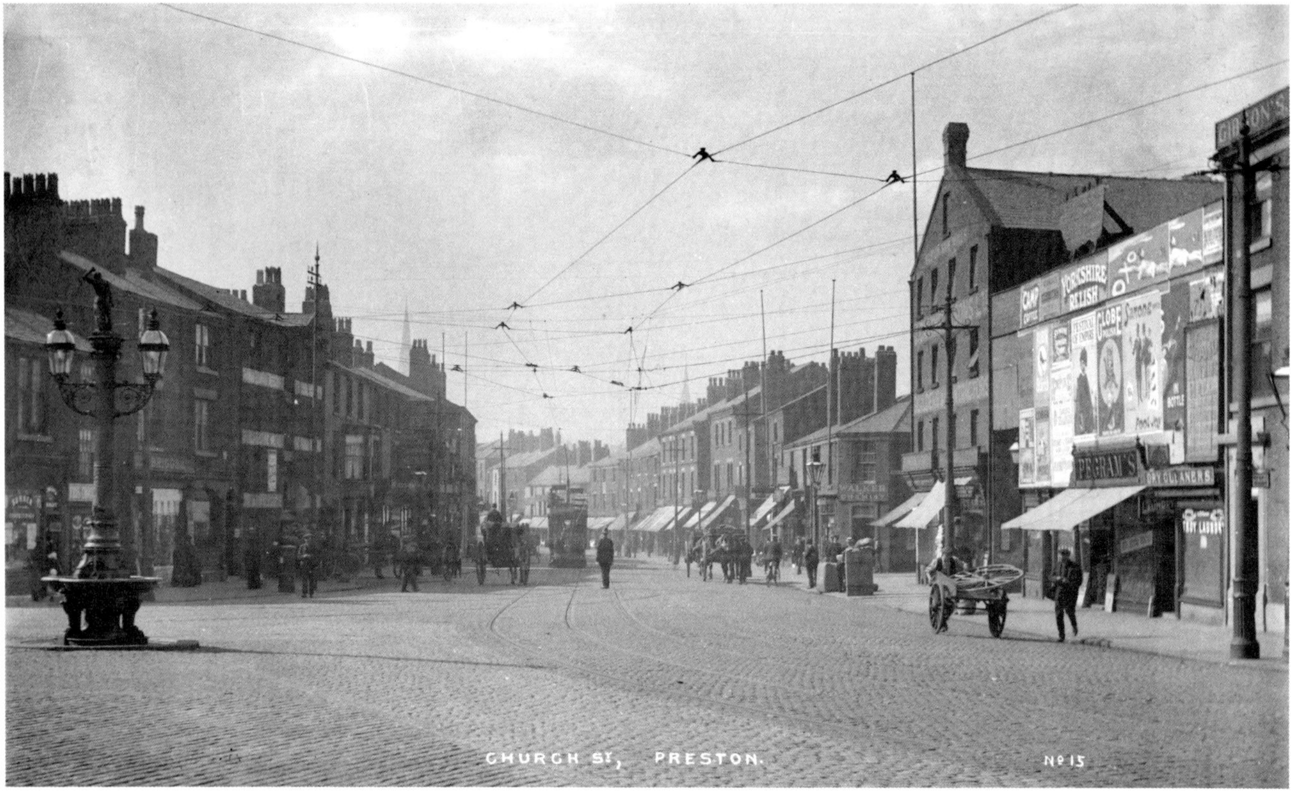

Church Street from Ribbleton Lane.

Across a sea of cobbles, a distant policeman stands immobile at the junction of Church Street, Park Road, Stanley Street and Ribbleton Lane; on the right a man slowly pushes a cart with two huge wheels on it; nearby, a man slowly steps off the pavement, oblivious that he is there. At the other side of the pavement is a block of property called Myerscough Buildings, almost entirely obscured by a huge hoarding, covered with dilapidated posters which advertise coffee, Yorkshire Relish and the wares of the Grand Clothing Hall, tailors, clothiers, and hatters of 56, Fishergate. Centrally placed beneath it is the Church Street branch of Pegrams, tea dealers; and, just to the right, The Troy Laundry and Carpet Beating Company. Just visible, to the right of Myerscough Buildings is the *Harp Inn*, and to the left, is a warehouse belonging to John Cartmell & Sons, joiners, builders, timber merchants and … undertakers' merchants! Across the entrance to Park Road is a two-storey building with a corner shop belonging to James Eteson Walker, chemist and druggist. Over on the left of the photograph is an unbelievably ugly drinking fountain that imagined itself to be a lamp post. It had obstructed the road there since the 1880s, and yet never seemed to have been noticed by anyone, not even when it vanished from the scene! A network of wires crowds the sky, providing the energy for Preston's new electric tramway system. It was only about five years old when this photograph was taken, but, so successful had it been that plans were being touted to expand the system to other towns. For Preston that was not to be, and the same system ran in the town until it closed in 1935. But now, at the turn of the twentieth and twenty first centuries, there is a revival of interest in the tram as a pollution free method of transport, and who knows, it may come back one day. Further down Church Street, things come to life, with numerous carts, a tram and a solitary cyclist turning up Park Road.

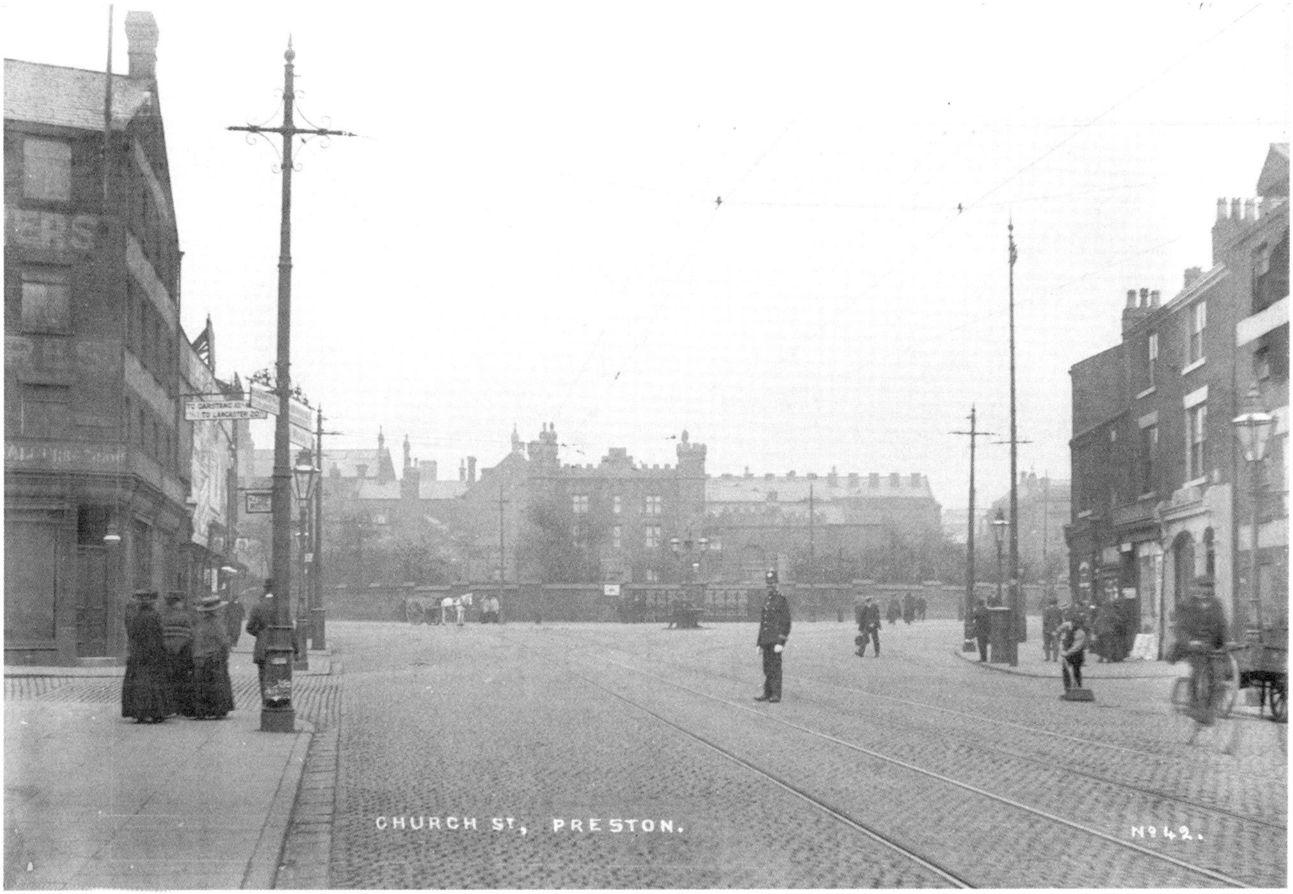

Church Street with the Governor's House and Preston Prison.

The years prior to the First World War represented the golden age of the postcard. Here, a policeman stands at ease, smiling, perhaps hoping that he will be included in a set of Shaw postcards. A sign GARSTANG 10 M / LANCASTER 23 M on the left of the photograph points towards Park Road, constructed in the early 19th century to enable traffic (horse-drawn of course) to head north without having to pass through the town centre. Park Road, which was named after the park which surrounded Sir Edward Stanley's residence, Patten House, in Church Street, still exists as the inner route of Ringway. Centrally placed in the photograph is the Prison, called the *House of Correction* when it was built in 1789. Fronting it is the castle-like *Governor's House*, built in 1834 during the Chartist Riots. Its two towers, complete with battlements, were intended to house cannon to fend off *'mobs of machinery-breaking cotton operatives'* who, only three years before, had stormed the prison in an attempt to free some of their supporters. The prison itself is a hallowed place, for on September 1, 1818 and again on October 25, 1820, Elizabeth Fry visited it with her brother, John Gurney. Fry had visited Newgate in 1813 and found there *'300 women, tried and untried, with their numerous children, herded together in filth and neglect'*. From that moment she resolved to devote her life to the welfare of prisoners. She was, however, very impressed by the *House of Correction* at Preston, expressing her admiration at the '*cleanliness and discipline observable in this place*'. Only one thing was wanting – *'more religious care and instruction'*.

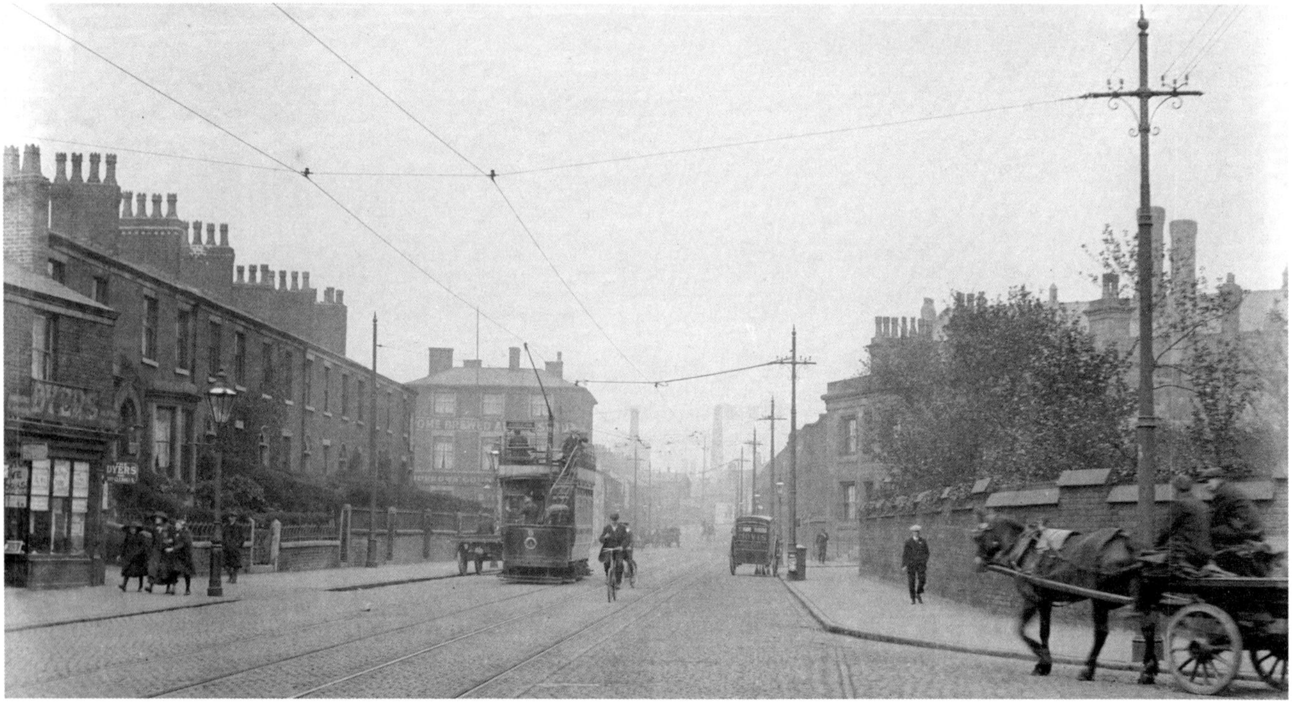

Ribbleton Lane from Church Street.

The Rev. John Clay, chaplain of Preston Prison, must regularly have walked home along the stretch of pavement on the right of the photograph. Clay had been appointed in 1821 following the recommendations of Elizabeth Fry and John Gurney who had visited the prison the previous year. Clay, unusually in his time, was recognised for his enlightened views on the treatment of prisoners. He was also known to Charles Dickens, who had met him at Parliamentary Committees on Prison Reform and during a visit he had made to Preston in 1854 to report on the strike of cotton operatives. One might therefore have expected that Dickens, whose novels highlight the terrible social inequalities of Victorian times, would have admired him. But no, his novel *Hard Times*, which is said to have been inspired by Preston and was published only a few months later in 1854, included the following unflattering portrait of Clay – *'Then came the experienced chaplain of the jail, with more tabular statements, outdoing all the previous tabular statements, and showing that the same people would resort to low haunts, hidden from the public eye, where they heard low singing and saw low dancing, and mayhap joined in it; and where A.B., aged twenty-four next birthday, and committed for eighteen months solitary, had himself said (not that he had ever shown himself worthy of belief) his ruin began, as he was perfectly sure and confident that otherwise he would have been a tip-top moral specimen'.* Shortly after its publication an irate Clay wrote to a Miss Carpenter – *'I see that Mr. Dickens, in Hard Times, has a laugh at my 'tabular statements' and also at my credulity. He is not the only man I have met with who prefers to rely on his own theories and fancies rather than on well ascertained facts'.* (!) On the left, above the level of the road, is a row of houses called *Mill Bank*, so called because a windmill stood on the site in the early 19th century. Tramcar No. 9 makes its way out of town along the Ribbleton Route. The conductor is manning the rear platform, which was his normal position when not collecting fares. It was also the best place for him to keep an eye on the trolley pole in case it became detached from the overhead electric wire; on these early tramway systems dewirements could and did occur. Flanking the road are the tramway electrical standards supporting the wires, many of which were still in place in the 1970s, having been modified to carry street lighting. Interestingly, in the photograph, tram No. 9, one of Preston's original trams of

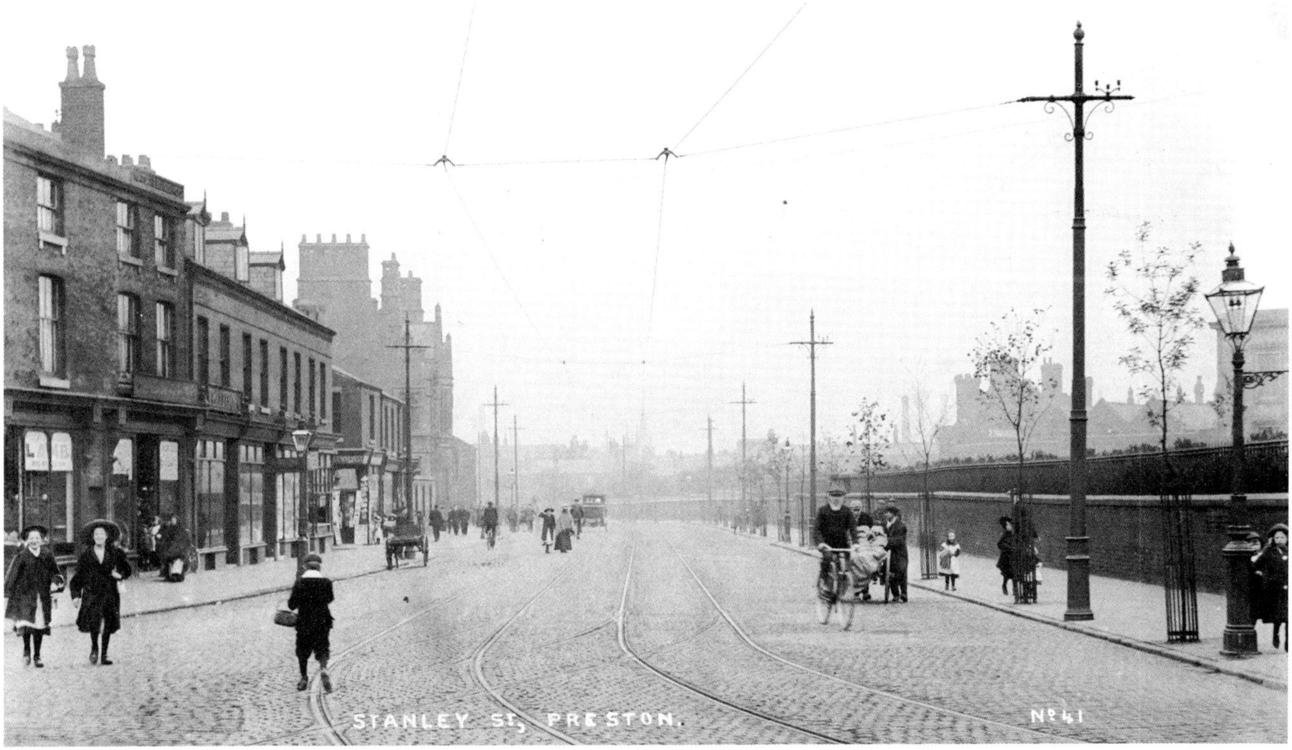

Stanley Street from New Hall Lane.

A young boy steps over a tram line in the road; a man on a bicycle overtakes a prematurely aged man carrying a load of cloth; and a distant trap and a couple of cyclists head for Church Street. How this leisurely scene contrasts with today, which sees a constant flow of traffic between Walton Bridge and Ringway. The large chimney stacks in the middle distance belong to the head office of Horrockses Crewdson & Company, situated at the entrance to the Yard Works, set up there by John Horrocks in 1791. In 1912, a new company office was constructed immediately to the left of the entrance. The Yard Works here was the great historic centre of the company; here it was that John Horrocks set up the *'Old Factory'* in 1791. At that time it relied for its motive power on a solitary horse drawing a central driving wheel round and round in a cellar; when this photograph was taken, the Yard Works had a gigantic horizontal beam engine capable of developing two thousand five hundred horse power! Beyond the trees on the right is Preston Prison with its Governor's House. Just visible, to the right of the lamp in the foreground, is the Court House, built in 1829, which was joined to the prison by a tunnel so that prisoners could be taken directly from the court to the cells. The first prison van used on the streets of Preston was in 1869.

1904, is still in its original open-top condition and has yet to receive the new top-cover that would later render it similar in appearance to No. 17, seen in one of the photographs of Broadgate. Many of these early tramcars had long careers and were progressively updated to protect passengers in bad weather and to incorporate newer refinements. No. 9 was to be no exception, and there exists a much later photograph showing it transformed as a totally enclosed car not only with top-cover but with upper and lower deck windscreens at each end, and still running when Preston's tramway system closed on December 15, 1935. But by that time, the last tram had already run on the Ribbleton route the previous year.

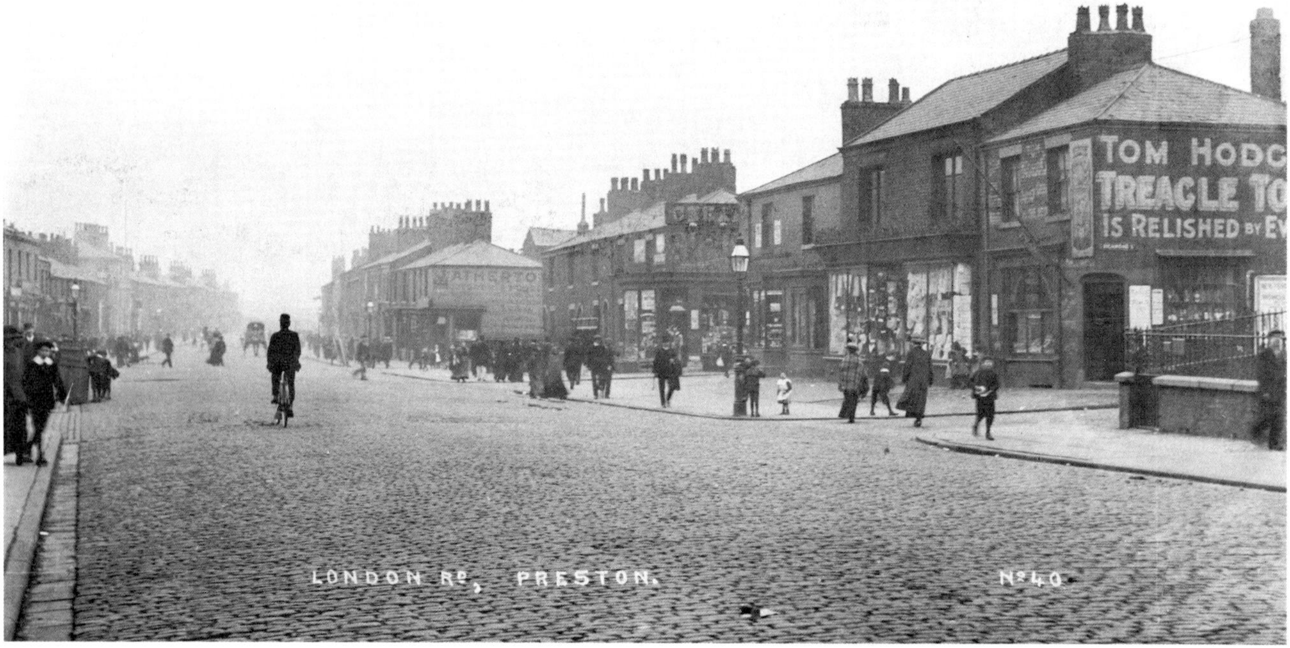

London Road from Richmond Street.

All the buildings on the right of this photograph were swept away in the town improvement schemes of the 1960s. A solitary cyclist freewheels down a cobbled London Road towards Walton Bridge. Most of the pedestrians are wearing their *'Sunday-best'*, and that is perhaps the day of the week that the Shaws have chosen to take their photograph. On the right, at the corner of Richmond Street is a barber's pole on the front of Christopher Halliwell's hairdresser's shop at No. 68, London Road. On the Richmond Street side, a huge advertisement – TOM HODGSON'S TREACLE TOFFEE IS RELISHED BY EVERYONE – has been painted on the brickwork of the house. This form of advertising was a popular feature on buildings in the years immediately prior to the First World War. Next door to Halliwell's is the double-fronted shop front of Butler and Hatfield, general drapers, ironmongers and house furnishers. Of the two remaining properties in this short block, one is a private house and the other, at the corner of Lark Hill Street, is William Neville's pawnbroker's shop. At the other corner is John Parkinson's grocer's shop, again with painted brickwork advertising SUNLIGHT SOAP. Above this on the roof is a large hoarding with the word CHEAP, which, if we could read the rest would probably say CHEAPEST. Just as the camera shutter clicks, a shop assistant, standing in the doorway, waves to two ladies on the pavement. Three private houses take us to Albyn Street East, where, across the road, John Atherton has built up a substantial retail business as a fishmonger, fruit, poultry and rabbit salesman, and florist at No. 88. And, of course, he also has a large painted advertisement on the side of his shop. All the property shown here on the right of the photograph has now been demolished, and in its place there is a modern housing estate. But it is people who make a picture; like the young boy, near the Richmond Street lamp-post, teasing a small child, perhaps with some of Tom Hodgson's treacle toffee, made in Accrington.

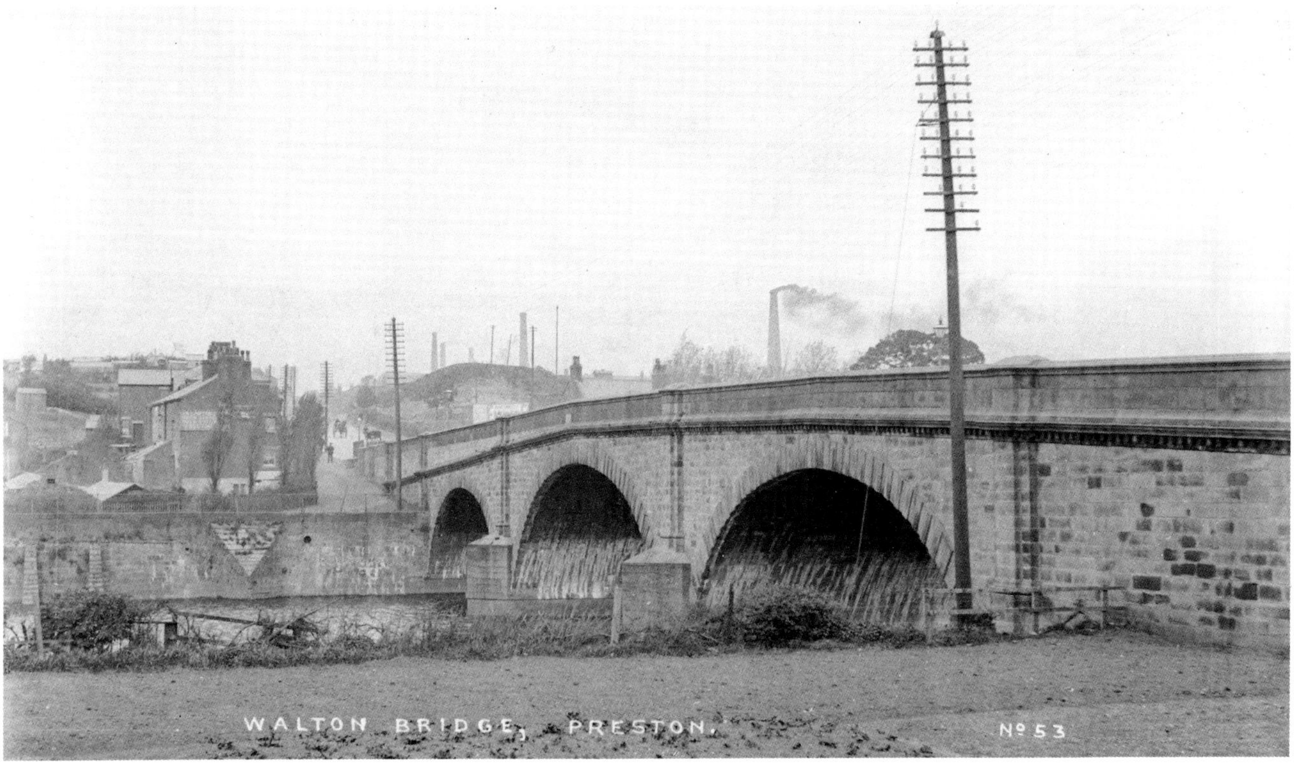

Walton Bridge from the Bridge Inn.

Bridges have spanned the River Ribble at Walton for over 700 years. That shown here was built by Samuel and Robert Laws, 1779-81, and cost £4,200. The bridge still exists and carries traffic on the upstream side from Preston to Walton. However, in 1936 the bridge was widened on the downstream side and the splendid architectural form shown here has vanished from view. Particularly interesting is the line of the parapet immediately over the arches, which clearly shows how hump-backed the bridge was in its early years. The first bridge, which dated from the reign of Henry III (1216-72), was situated a little downstream on a line near the left edge of the photograph. One of the most ferocious battles of the Civil War took place here on August 17, 1648, when the Royalists, in Cromwell's own words, *"were beaten from the bridge; and our horse and foot, following them, killed many and took divers prisoners"*. The old bridge was demolished in 1782 and only on rare occasions, when the water is very low, can the last traces of it be seen.

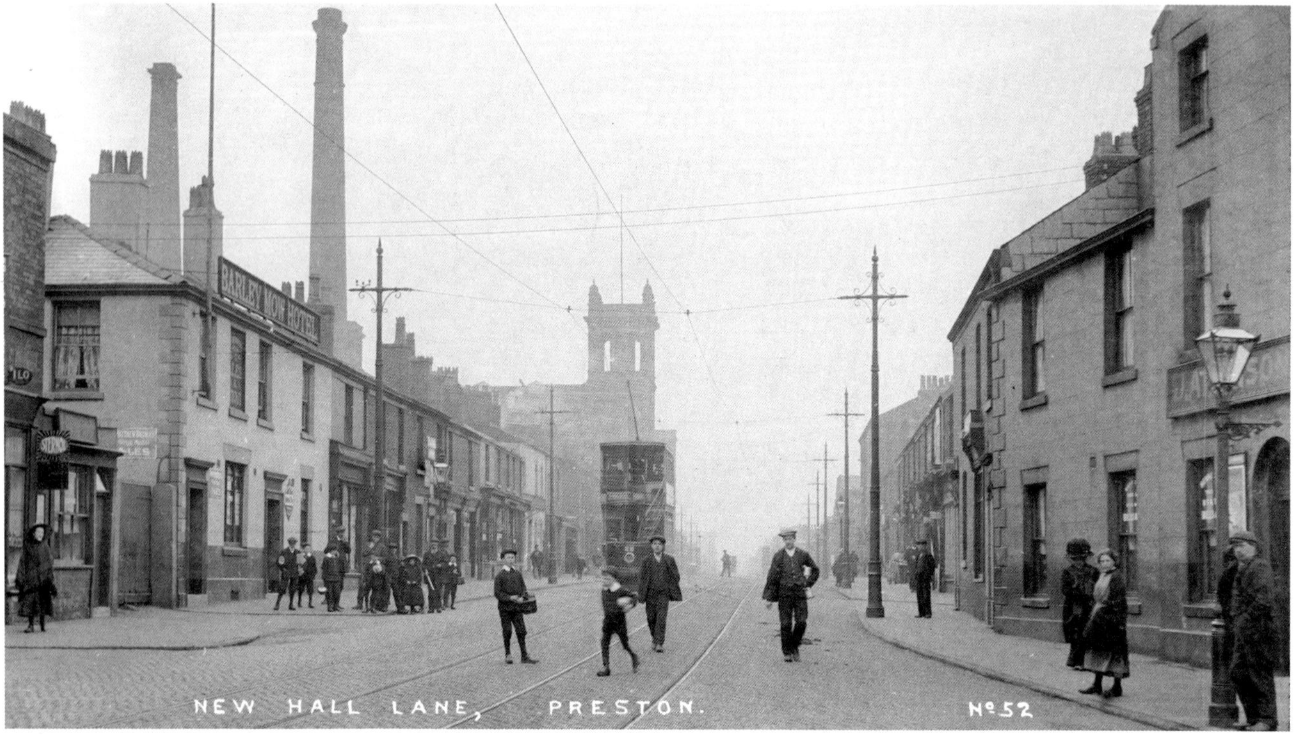

New Hall Lane from Stanley Street.

New Hall Lane is a medieval road which became a new highway to Preston when the turnpike road was constructed in 1824-25. It took on its built-up appearance in 1803 when John Horrocks constructed homes for his cotton operatives in this western section and its adjoining streets and called the district 'New Preston'. Writing in 1869, Anthony Hewitson, editor of the *Preston Guardian*, described this district as almost beyond the reach of the law – *'Hand loom weaving is now about as hopeless a job as trying to extract sunlight out of cucumbers; but at that time (the 1830s) it was a paying affair. Weavers could afford to play two or three days a week, earn excellent wages, afterwards wear top boots and then thrash their wives in comfort without the interference of policemen. They and their immediate descendants belonged to a crooked and perverse generation. Cock fighting, badger baiting, poaching, drinking and dog worrying found their sovereign delights, and they were so amazingly rude and dangerous that even tax collectors durst not at times, go amongst them for money… The population has thickened and civilisation has penetrated into the region since then, and yet the 'animal' preponderates rather largely in it now. Rats, pigeons, dogs and Saturday night eye openers, toned down with canary breeding, ale-supping, herb gathering and Sunday afternoon baking – still retain a mild hold upon the affections of the people, and many of the youthful race are beginning to imitate their elders admirably in all these little particulars. A pack of hounds was once kept for general enjoyment in New Preston, but that pack has 'gone to the dogs' – hasn't been heard of for years'.* Many of the houses have now been rebuilt, but the Shaws' magnificent photographs give us a glimpse of the district which dates back to the beginning of Preston's Industrial Revolution. Just visible on the right is the *Rose Bud* public house which dates from 1869. To the left is the *Barley Mow* public house, which opened in the 1850s and still survives as a yacht chandler's. The shops beyond it housed drapers, cloggers, confectioners, herbalists and a hairdresser's when this photograph was taken. On the left of the picture, a group of children and adults stand to watch the photographer. Could it be that they have just alighted from the tram that pulls away up New Hall Lane?

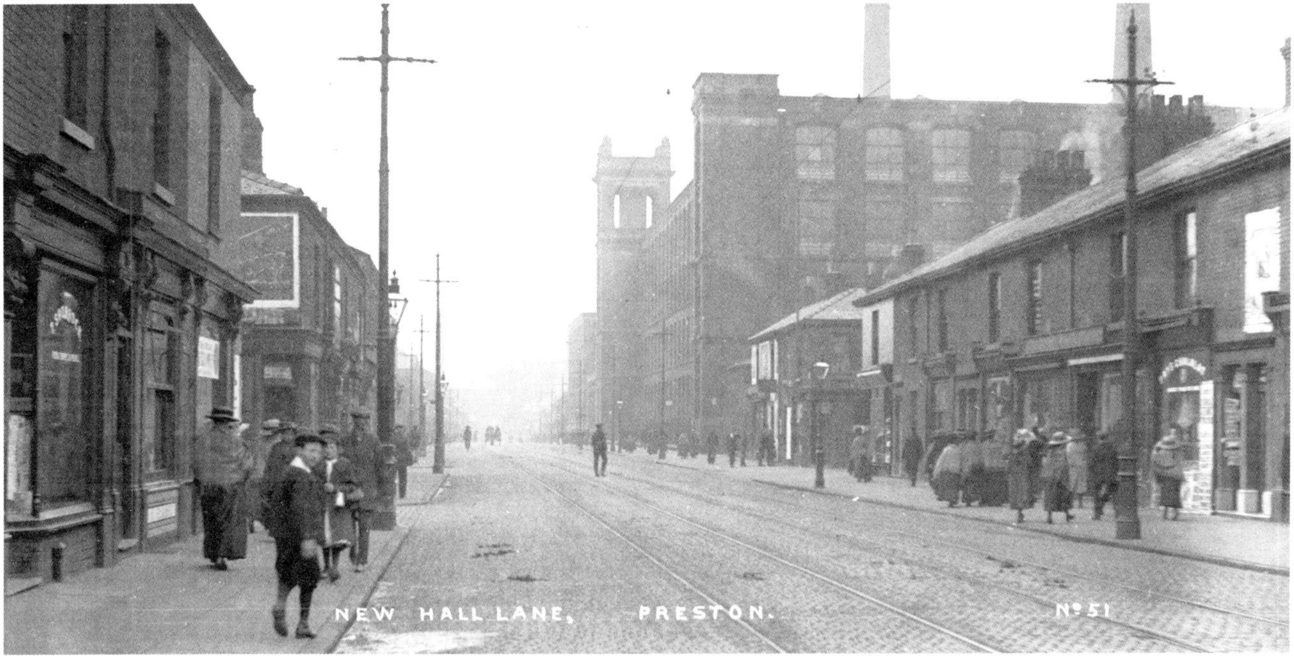

New Hall Lane with Horrockses' Centenary Mill.

John Horrocks is one of the mighty founding fathers of cotton manufacture. From his early beginnings in the *'Old Factory'*, Dale Street, in 1791, he built up an industry which, at the time this photograph was taken, employed over 6,000 workpeople; had engines amounting to 12,800 horse power, which drove 330,000 spindles and 8,500 looms; and had a weekly output of cloth over 600 miles long! That was the heyday of the cotton industry; now the Centenary Mill, built in 1891 as a triumphant celebration of the might of Horrockses Crewdson & Company, is still and silent. Just as important in a history of the world's industry is Henrietta street, which once opened on to New Hall Lane just beyond the massive arcaded tower near the entrance to Centenary Mill, and part of which is still accessible from the nearby St. Mary's Street. It all goes back to March 8, 1832, when a John Huntington was born in Everton Gardens, a road which ran parallel with Tithebarn Street and is now under the concrete apron of the Central Bus Station. In 1852, at the age of twenty, he became a grinder in the cardroom of Seed's Mill in Ribbleton, where he earned 9s. 6d per week. He married a June Beck, who earned 10s. 0d per week as a weaver at Horrockses; and they set up home at 2, Henrietta Street. A year later, Huntington found himself elected as one of the strike leaders in the Great Lockout at Preston. When the strike ended, Huntington was blacklisted and decided to emigrate to America. He and his family travelled west to Cleveland, Ohio, where he set up as a builder. One day he saw a *'For Sale'* sign on a pig and poultry farm and decided to buy it. The rest is the stuff of dreams – the stench of the farm was not the pigs or the poultry, but oil. John Huntington, who had lived in Henrietta Street among the ragged half-starved cotton operatives of New Preston, had just found himself the owner of one of the largest oil fields that was ever to be discovered. He later was to join John D. Rockefeller in founding the Standard Oil Company, more popularly known as *Esso*. Huntington never lost touch with his home town; on August 27, 1882, as part of the Guild celebrations, he attended St. Paul's Church for the opening ceremony of a new baptistery, for which he had paid £2,500. John Huntington died on January 10, 1893, leaving a fortune of $1,300,00 dollars; but for the people in this photograph, perhaps the children and grandchildren of mill workers who had known Huntington and his wife, life was little better than it had been when he left. On the right, a group of women in long skirts, and almost completely hidden by their hats (!), slowly make their way past a shop selling Fry's chocolate.

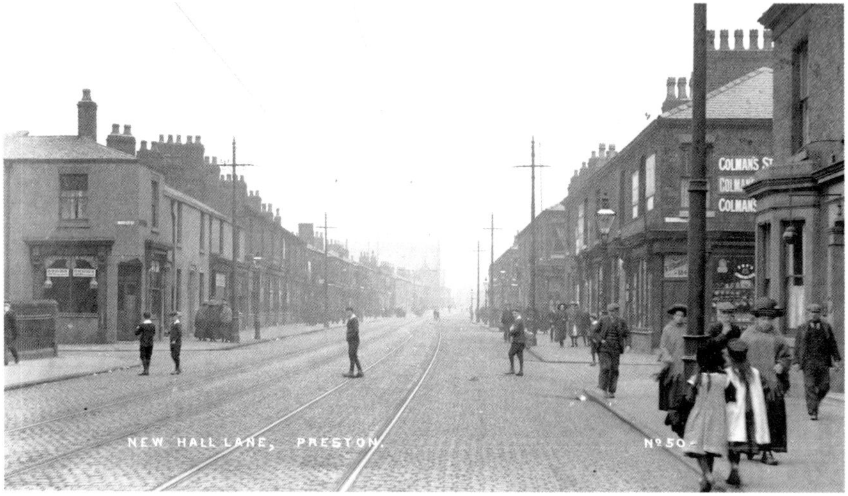

New Hall Lane looking east.

In 1861, Preston was unfortunate enough to attract the attention of a correspondent in the *Builder* magazine, writing about sanitation in northern industrialised towns. No part of the town was spared, and it made cruel reading for members of the Town Council who were clearly taken off guard. The correspondent visited this very scene and wrote:- *'More mills, and more mud; a row of houses, with a man weaving in a cellar in one of them; a great stagnant swamp, with a brick yard in it, and a square dung heap; an isolated row of houses in Skeffington-road, with pools of drainage spread before them; more mills, more mud, more dwellings propped up while building, with five feet of drainage water in the cellars and a foul ditch in the rear; then a length of blighted trees, blighted hedges, and foul ditches, on either side of the coal-ash road; cows grazing in fields where there are stagnant pools and the grass is tinged with an unearthly green'.* We can thank the anonymous writer of the article for having galvanised Preston Corporation into improving the lot of the people living in this and other districts of the town in the succeeding years.

Cemetery Gates, New Hall Lane.

It was only in the 1880s that the eastern part of New Hall Lane beyond Skeffington Road began to be built on. Before that, this stretch of the lane was surrounded by fields, with a good view of the hills across the Ribble valley on the south side. However, at the cemetery gates there was the present *Hesketh's Arms* public house, and the two lodges shown flanking the gates. Our correspondent travelled in this direction, from Skeffington Road towards the cemetery, about a mile out of town, which had been opened in 1855, – *'Then it is that we count funerals in front of us, funerals behind us, funerals keeping pace with us; mourners dressed in black are passing along the black footways; the hedges, ditches, and sheep in the fields, are all black; the smoke blowing from the factories and hovering over the roads, now eddying, now descending in flakes, is also black; and it becomes difficult to shake off the impression that we are being carried to the grave ourselves … We come to a group of ecclesiastical domestic buildings and the cemetery gates. We take the former to be the superintendent's lodge, but we are mistaken. It is the 'Hesketh Arms and Cemetery Hotel'! For a hotel to be close to the lodge and entrance gates of a spacious cemetery of fifty acres, with three chapels in it, is an innovation for which we were not prepared'.* At that time there was no Blackpool Road, which was only constructed from 1926 onwards; only the lane, which continued on past the cemetery to Brockholes Brow and down to the Halfpenny Bridge.

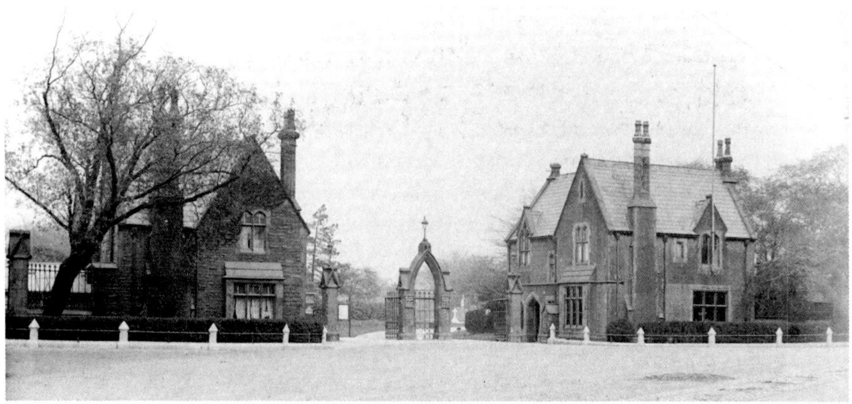

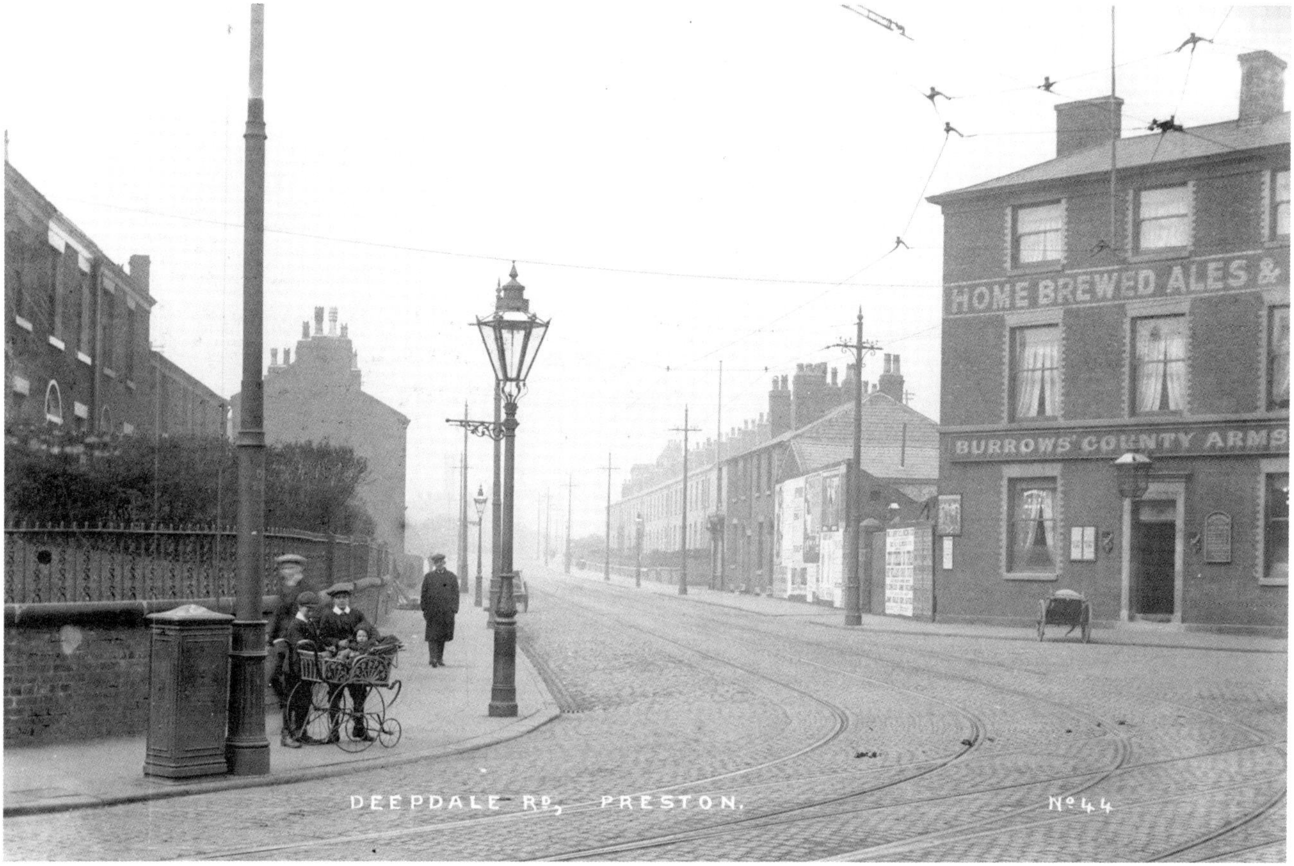

Deepdale Road from Ribbleton Lane.

It is not history that catches our eye in this photograph, but an evocative group of two young men, in Sunday best, wearing caps, fustian suits and shining boots, looking after a young child in an extraordinary pram that has no tyres on its metal wheels. Here at the junction of Deepdale Road is Albert Burrows' *County Arms*, an early 19th century public house which dates from the 1820s and certainly must have been known to the Rev. John Clay, Chaplain of Preston Prison, and, who knows, may have been one of the *'low haunts'* with *'low singing'* and *'low dancing'* that Charles Dickens 'quotes' him, in *Hard Times*, as having deplored so much! Coal was the driving force behind Preston's cotton industry, as well as a source of fuel for the thousands of back-to-back houses in the town. Here, obscured from view by the *County Arms* and a large hoarding advertising local theatrical performances, is Deepdale Sidings, accessed by a branch of the West Riding Junction Railway to Longridge, which had been opened in 1840. The sidings, with its mountains of coal, supplied Preston's needs through the wholesale coal and coke merchants who had their premises there – the Wigan Coal & Iron Company, Thomas Banks, Colliery Agent, and Thomas Bamber, John Jackson & Sons, James Martin, and Thomas Maymon and Sons, coal and coke dealers – small wonder that a vast cloud of smoke and smog, pouring out from the factory chimneys and domestic dwellings, was an ever-present feature of the Preston landscape.

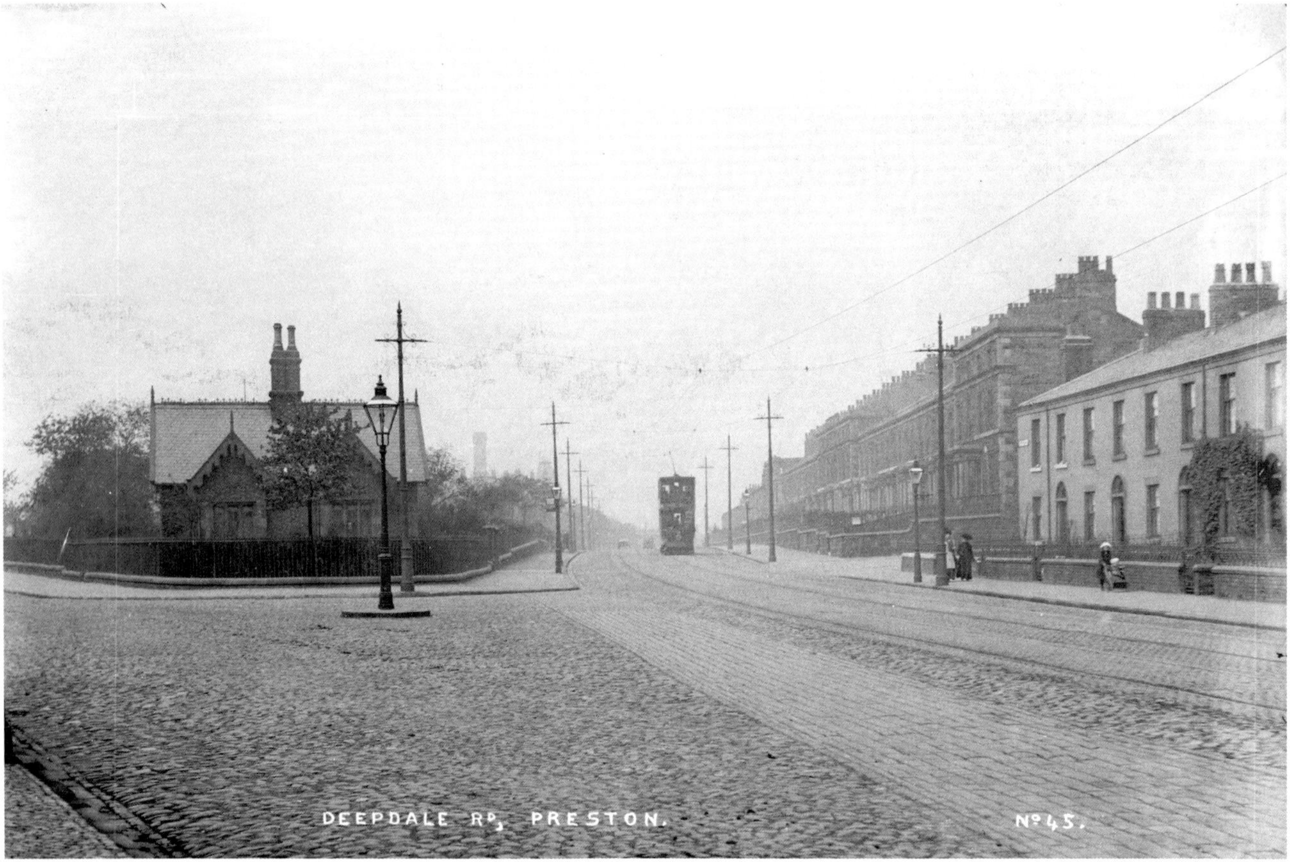

Deepdale Road from Stephenson Terrace.

On the left of the photograph is Deepdale Enclosure, which was elevated to the status of a park on January 29, 1881. In the 18th century, this triangle of land bounded by Deepdale Road, East View and Meadow Street, comprised three fields named *'Cuckstool Pit Meadow'*, *'Further Cuckstool Pit Meadow'* and *'Cuckstool Meadow'*, and was the place where *'mischievous tongued women'* and on occasion debtors were punished in a ducking stool. The gabled cottage, built in 1850, was the Gardener's Lodge, owned by Thomas Lambert when this photograph was taken. In 1881, Preston Corporation purchased a telescope for £100 from a local amateur astronomer, Alderman Robert Watson, and set it up in an observatory in the enclosure. The same telescope was again moved, to the present observatory in Moor Park, just in time to view the total eclipse of the sun on June 29, 1927. On a raised elevation to the right is Stephenson Terrace, built by contractor George Mould in 1849 and named after the famous engineer. Advancing along a line of tramway electrical standards, a tram grinds its way down the slope towards Ribbleton Lane. The advent of the tram brought a network of wires in the sky and massive street furniture which dwarfed the lamp-posts of an earlier age.

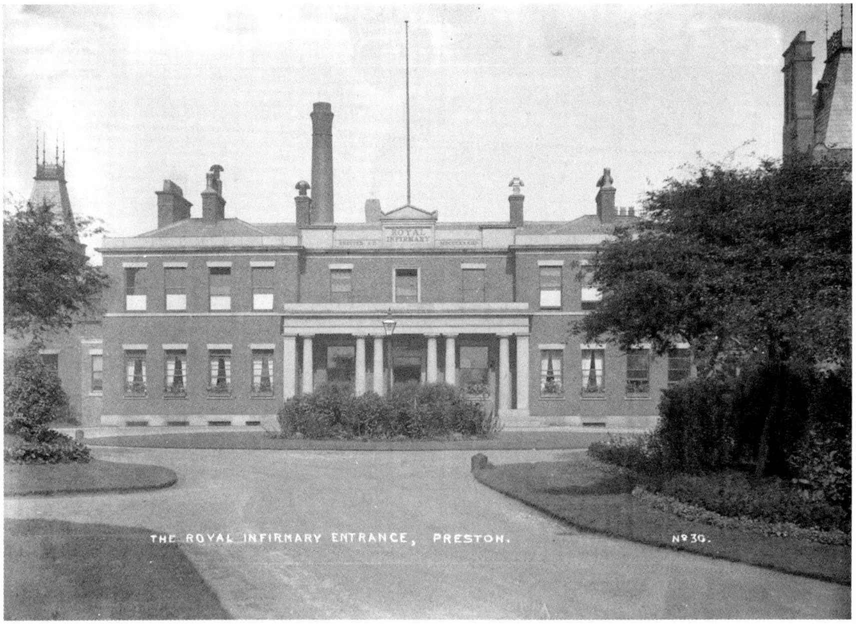

Preston Royal Infirmary, Central Administrative Building.

As long ago as the 13th century a leper hospital stood on the site of the present St. Walburge's Church. Dedicated to St. Mary Magdalen, the hospital gave its name to the district, *Maudlands* (or Magdalen lands), in which the church stands. However, the immediate ancestor of the present hospital system is the building shown in the photograph on the left, used as the administrative block in the former Preston Royal Infirmary in Deepdale Road. Originally called the *House of Recovery*, it was erected in 1833. When the Infirmary was transferred to Fulwood some years ago, this building, together with other parts of the Infirmary, was converted into residential housing units.

Preston Royal Infirmary.

The photograph on the right shows the early administrative section centrally placed between later hospital wings occupying a pleasant situation on Deepdale Road. In November 1876 fever wards were opened in detached blocks at the rear of the building for scarlet and enteric fever, as well as smallpox cases. This was followed in 1884 by the opening of a children's ward. To celebrate the Diamond Jubilee of Queen Victoria, funds were raised which resulted in important additions, including a Nurses' Home, Out-Patients' Department and an Operating Theatre. In 1909, at about the time this picture was taken, the number of patients in the hospital was 1,475.

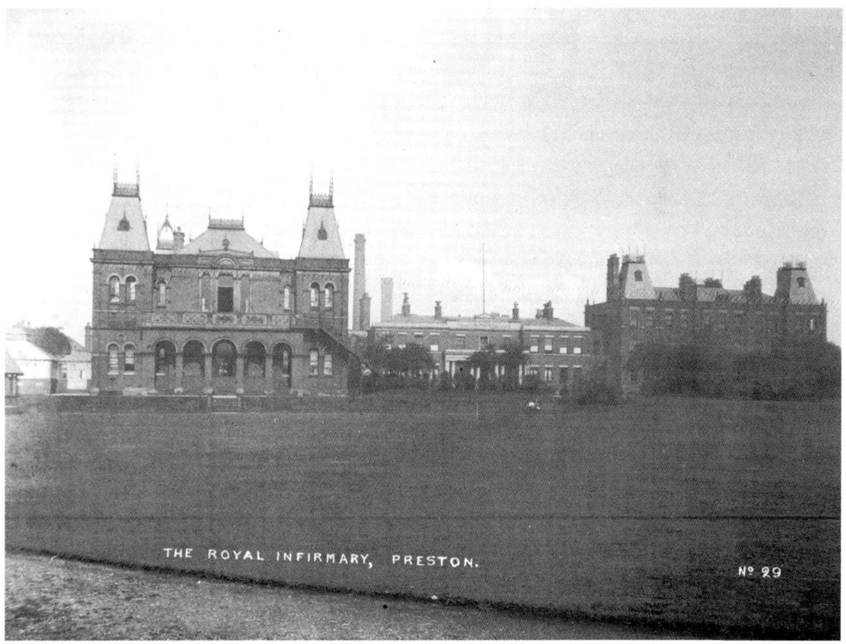

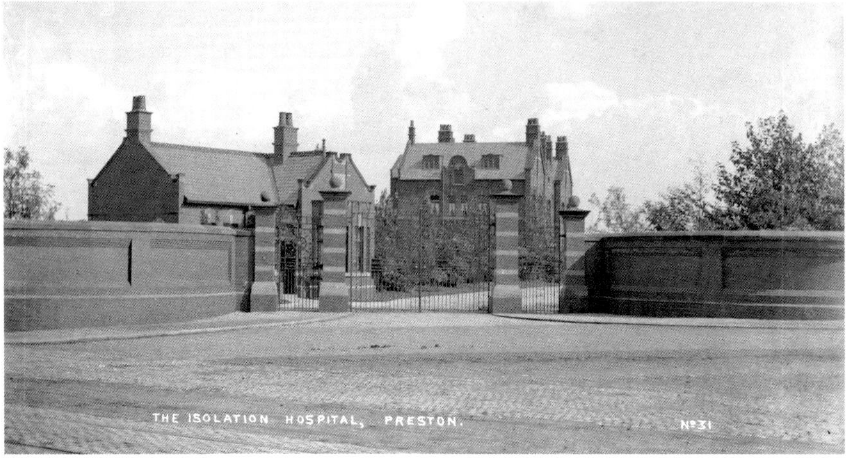

The Isolation Hospital, Deepdale Road (or Sir Tom Finney Way).

The New Year celebrations for 1903 were accompanied by an alarming outbreak of smallpox in the Avenham district. Amidst the distress, soup kitchens were set up in Manchester Road to alleviate the suffering of the people. It was the latest in a series of outbreaks of infectious killer diseases which had hit the crowded and insanitary districts of Preston. As early as November 1876, fever wards had been opened at the Royal Infirmary, but after the outbreak of 1903 there were calls for a special, purpose-built hospital to deal with such diseases. In 1907, a new Isolation Hospital opened at the junction of Deepdale Road and Serpentine Road (later to become part of the new Blackpool Road in the 1920s). When this photograph was taken it had 22 bedrooms and 4 ward pavilions, 2 for scarlet fever, 1 for diphtheria, and one for typhoid, as well as a laundry, disinfecting house and mortuary. Here it is, silent and deserted, surrounded by high walls and secure wrought iron gates to keep the public away from the dread diseases.

Fulwood Barracks, Watling Street Road.

Fulwood Barracks, on Watling Street Road, was built in 1843-8, and enlarged in 1856-7. It can be no coincidence that when there was civil strife, in 1842, with the Chartists, and in 1854, with the Preston Strike, the authorities strengthened the position of the army in Preston. Here we see the entrance to the barracks, with an iron balustraded drive which gives the impression of a moated entrance to a castle! High up on the huge archway, which was sadly demolished some years ago, is an outstanding and magnificent Royal coat-of-arms. This has been preserved and can now be seen on the ground at the entrance to the barracks. It was carved by Thomas Duckett, a native of Preston, who was one of the most accomplished sculptors of his time. He is best known for the very fine sculpture of Sir Robert Peel in Winckley Square, which was said at the time to be the finest likeness ever made of the statesman. He also intended to execute a colossal sculpture of Sir Richard Arkwright, the great pioneer of cotton industry, who had been born in Preston. He even made a full scale plaster model of how it was going to look. Unfortunately, funds could not be found and eventually his model was broken up, a sad loss to Preston. Through the archway two soldiers are on sentry duty, one of whom is watching the photographer very closely; not surprisingly because a dominating item in the newspapers of the day was home rule for Ireland.

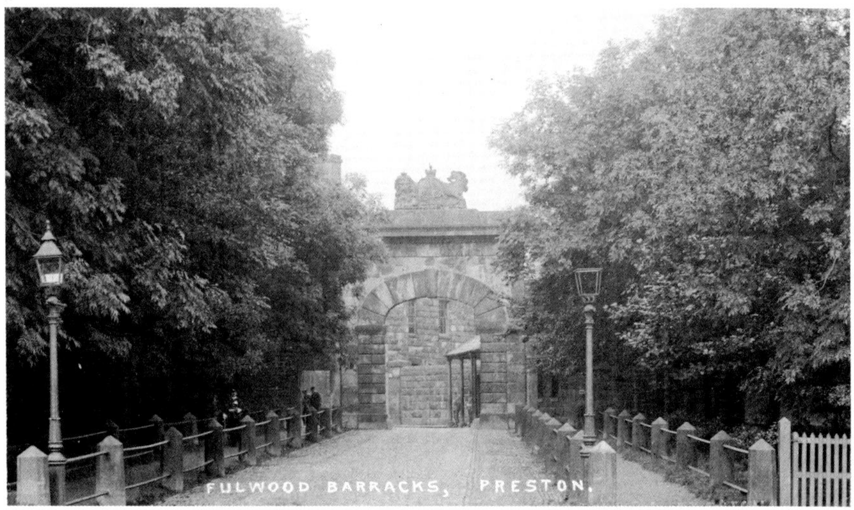

Fishergate with Old Town Hall.

In 1821, Whittle, a historian of Preston, wrote that *'Fishergate may truly be called the most genteel part of Preston'*. The reason for this was that many of its buildings were the private houses of the Lancashire aristocracy. The shopocracy which followed, divided and subdivided the original dwellings, converting them into places of business. But something of the old gentility survives in this photograph, which must be one of the finest ever taken of Fishergate. Interestingly, the flagging of Preston's pavements commenced on November 24, 1821. On the left is the Gothic façade and wedge-shaped tower of Preston Gas Company (known as *The Gas Offices*), pulled down to make way for the Fishergate entrance to St. George's Shopping Centre. To its left, the lines of the pavement lead to Chapel Walks, constructed in 1726 to allow access to St. George's Church. It was only about 1810 that a more direct route, Lune Street, was opened up to Fishergate. A boy helps his friend replace the chain on his cycle outside Preston Cycling Club, which had its headquarters through the archway of the *Shelley Arms*. But look at the club's sign – what is happening over it? A man stands on a parapet, but he hasn't got a ladder!!

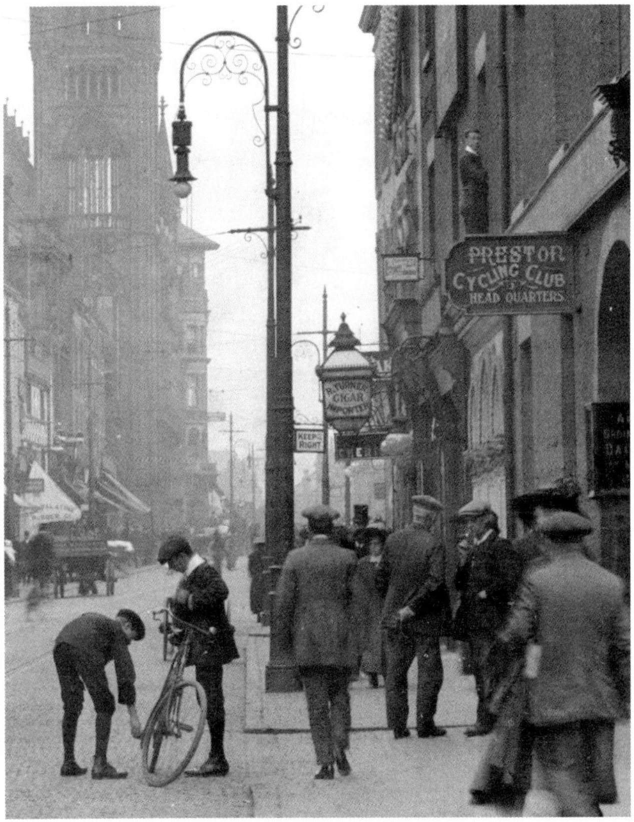

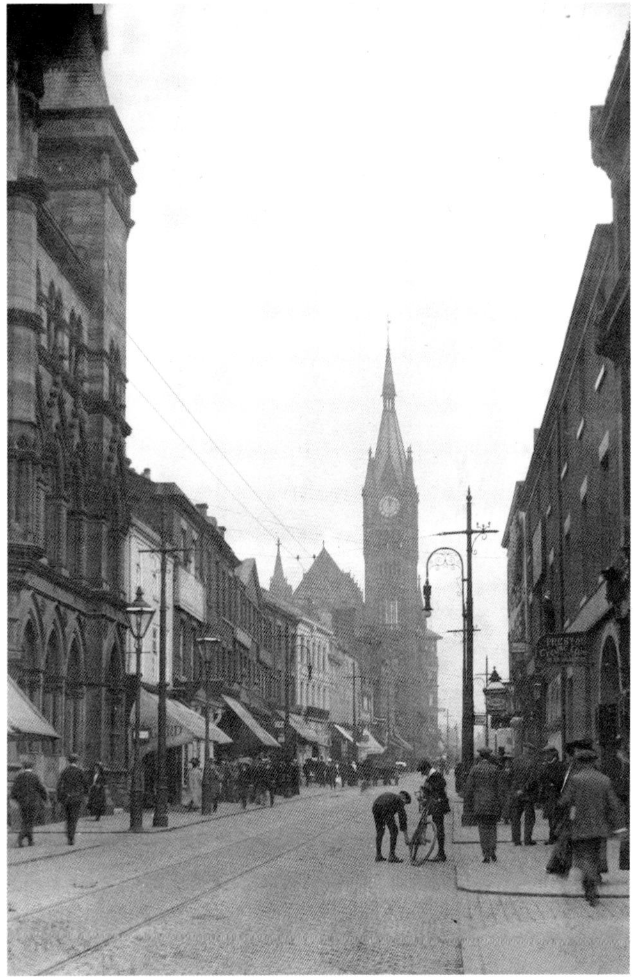

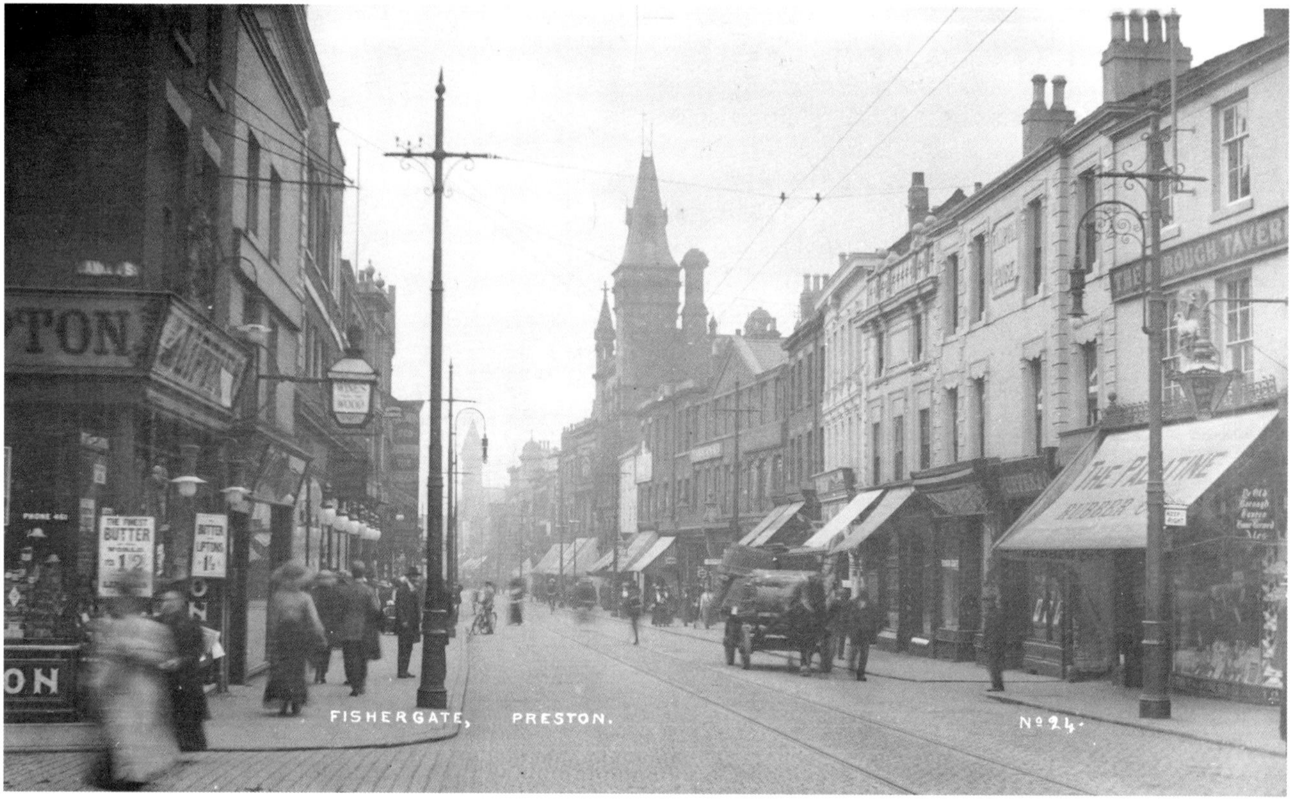

Fishergate from Guildhall Street.

Fishergate is said to be as old as Preston itself. However, since it follows the route leading from Clitheroe to the most downstream ford of the River Ribble at Penwortham Holme, it may be even older. It derives its name from being the main route to the river from Preston, and highlights the importance of the Ribble salmon fisheries in medieval times. On the left, at the corner of Cannon Street, is Lipton's, high class tea and provision merchants and wine and spirit dealers, with a sign in the window THE FINEST BUTTER IN THE WORLD. This is a site with an interesting history; in 1830 it was occupied by Huffman, a clogger. He is remembered for an episode during the Preston Election of 1830, when he punched the radical candidate, Henry *'Orator'* Hunt, in the face; more embarrassingly, it was in Hunt's own headquarters, the *Grey Horse* (now *Yates's Wine Lodge*, opposite Lancaster Road). No, he was not a supporter of Sir Edward Stanley, the Whig candidate; apparently, he did not think that Hunt was radical enough! On the right is the old *Borough Tavern* (now Samuel's jewellers); just beyond it is an alley way that led to Beethams, joiners. Further away, in the photograph, is a group of light coloured buildings, demolished to make way for the new Marks and Spencer's store in 1929. The furthest away of the three is at a slight angle to the other two, and this can clearly be seen in Marks and Spencer's façade to the present day. Rising up on the skyline is the wedge-shaped tower of the Fishergate headquarters of Preston Gas Company. It was founded as early as 1815 by the Rev. Fr. Dunn, S.J. (1746-1827), who is remembered nationally as one of the great pioneers of the use of coal-gas. Father Joseph Dunn, or *'Daddy'* Dunn as he was popularly known locally, headed the Catholic mission to Preston at St. Wilfrid's Church, Chapel Street, from 1775 until his death in 1827. When this photograph was taken, the company had 27,500 meters in use, and an annual consumption of 485,000,000 cubic feet of gas. The price to consumers was 3s. $5^3/_4$d. per 1,000 cubic feet.

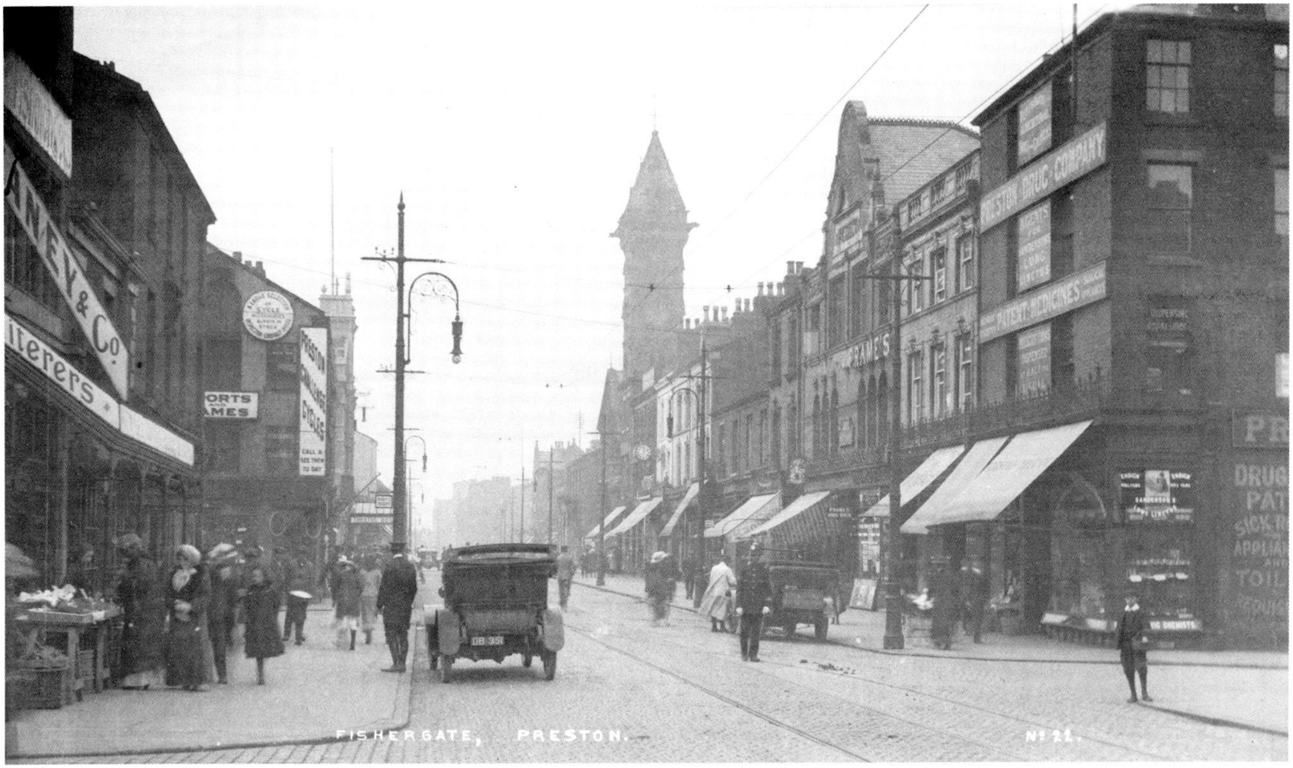

Fishergate from Chapel Street.

On the left is Heaney & Co., fruiterers, florists, fishmongers, game and poultry dealers, established in 1869, who had over their doorway the Royal coat of arms - *By Appointment to Queen Victoria*. This was a very exclusive establishment, patronised by all the leading families at the time, as can be seen by the splendid new motor car outside the premises. Its number plate DB 351, suggests that the chauffeur, standing alongside it on the pavement, had brought the owner from Stockport, Cheshire, where it was registered. In later years Heaney's premises were occupied by Macfisheries who carried on the business to the same standards as their predecessors. Across the road at the corner of Fox Street, is Preston Drug Company, *'dealers in photographic requisites, drug, spice and chemical merchants, patent medicine importers, sick-room appliances and toilet requisites'*. They were also agents for Sanderson's Lung Linctus, and were able to offer their customers *'Prescriptions dispensed at half the usual prices'* – too good to be true!! Further away, on the same side, is a Dutch gabled red-brick building, the premises of Frame's travel agents, run by John Frame, tourist, excursion, and shipping agent, *'also at London, Liverpool, Edinburgh, and Glasgow'*. Silhouetted against the sky is Fishergate Baptist Church, opened on July 1, 1858. It was designed by James Hibbert, architect of the Harris Library and Museum, in what they called at that time the Byzantine style, but in actuality is Italian Romanesque with Moorish additions. The church is one of the most architecturally important buildings in Preston, singled out by the Victorian art critic, John Ruskin, for the naturalistic carved foliage on its façade, and also admired by the architect, Sir George Gilbert Scott, who regularly visited Preston in the 1860s to see progress on his new Town Hall. On November 26, 1860, the Rev. F. Bugby, first minister of Fishergate Baptist Church, presented a Bible to a Mr and Mrs W. Cowell on the occasion of their marriage, the first to be held there. Some years ago, the descendants of Mr and Mrs Cowell returned it to the church, where it is still used on special occasions.

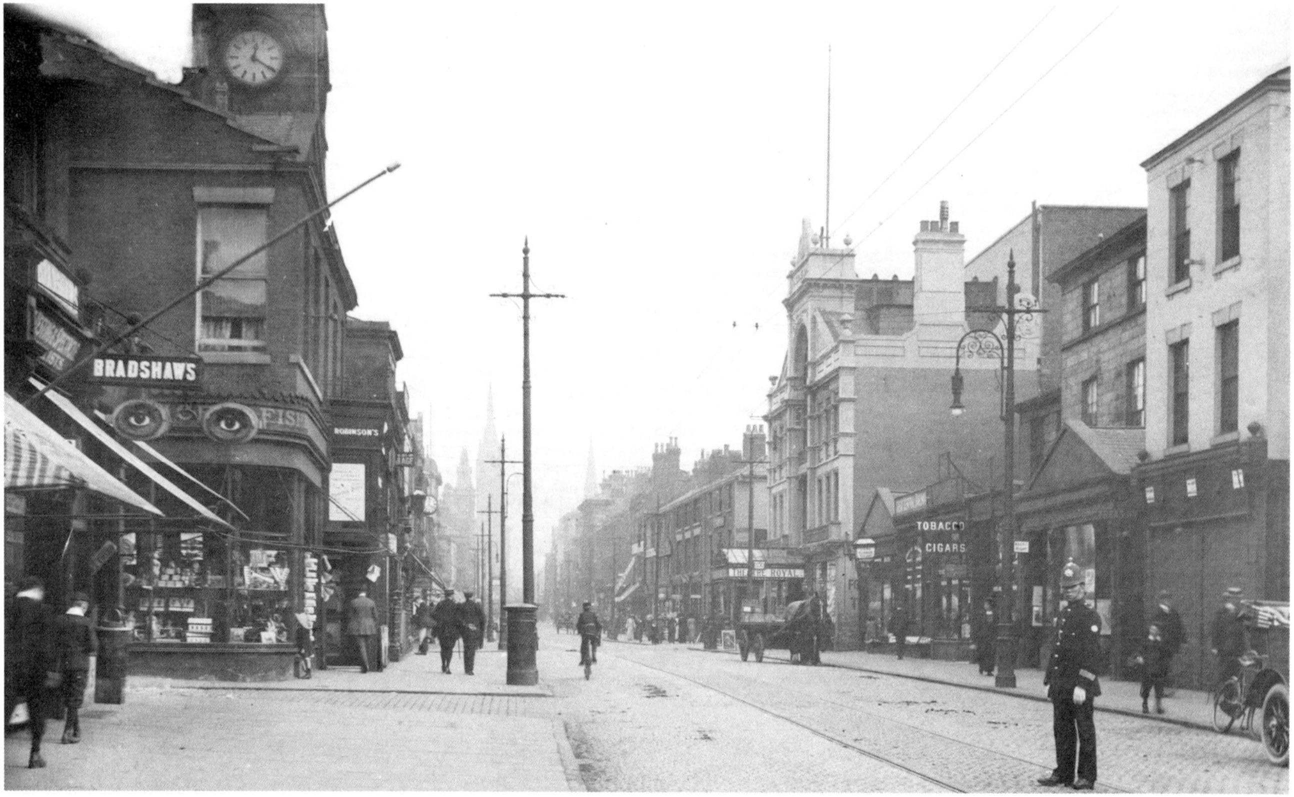

Fishergate with the Theatre Royal.

Preston has always had a strong association with the theatre. Thomas Preston, the dramatist who wrote *Cambyses, King of Persia*, was born here on August 13, 1530. In its own time the play was regarded as overbearingly bombastic in its use of language, and was actually lampooned by Shakespeare in Henry IV, Part 1, ii. iv: *'I must speak in passion, and I will do it in King Cambyses' vein'*. It is not known where the town's playhouse was in those early days, but in the 1760s it occupied an old Friends Meeting House in Woodcock's Yard, now occupied by the HMV shop in Fishergate. It may have been as manager of those premises that the eminent actor, John Philip Kemble (1757-1823), elder brother of two equally famous actors, Charles Kemble and Mrs Siddons, was appointed in 1793. However, it was in 1802 that Preston gained its first purpose-built theatre, in the *Theatre Royal*, Fishergate. Here we see it after a later rebuilding in 1898. Immediately to the right is a one-storey high line of shops, then called *'The Arcade'*, which was built over the front garden of the mansion of William Cartwright, designer of the old tramway which joined the northern and southern sections of the Lancaster Canal by a line that ran through Avenham Park and over the Old Tram Bridge. The general lines of the mansion and arcade can still be seen as part of Littlewood's store in Fishergate Shopping Centre. The shops in the arcade include one with the sign TOBACCO CIGARS, which advertises the premises of Backhouse & Sons. Immediately to its left, on the roof line, is the sign of the office of the Great Central Railway Co. On the far left of the photograph is a barber's pole, advertising the premises of Robert Bomont, hairdresser, of 3, Victoria Buildings. Next door is a huge pair of spectacles incorporating hypnotic eyes, belonging not surprisingly to Bradshaw's opticians. But what of the policeman in the middle of the road? Is he directing traffic at that spot, or is he keeping a wary eye on the photographer?

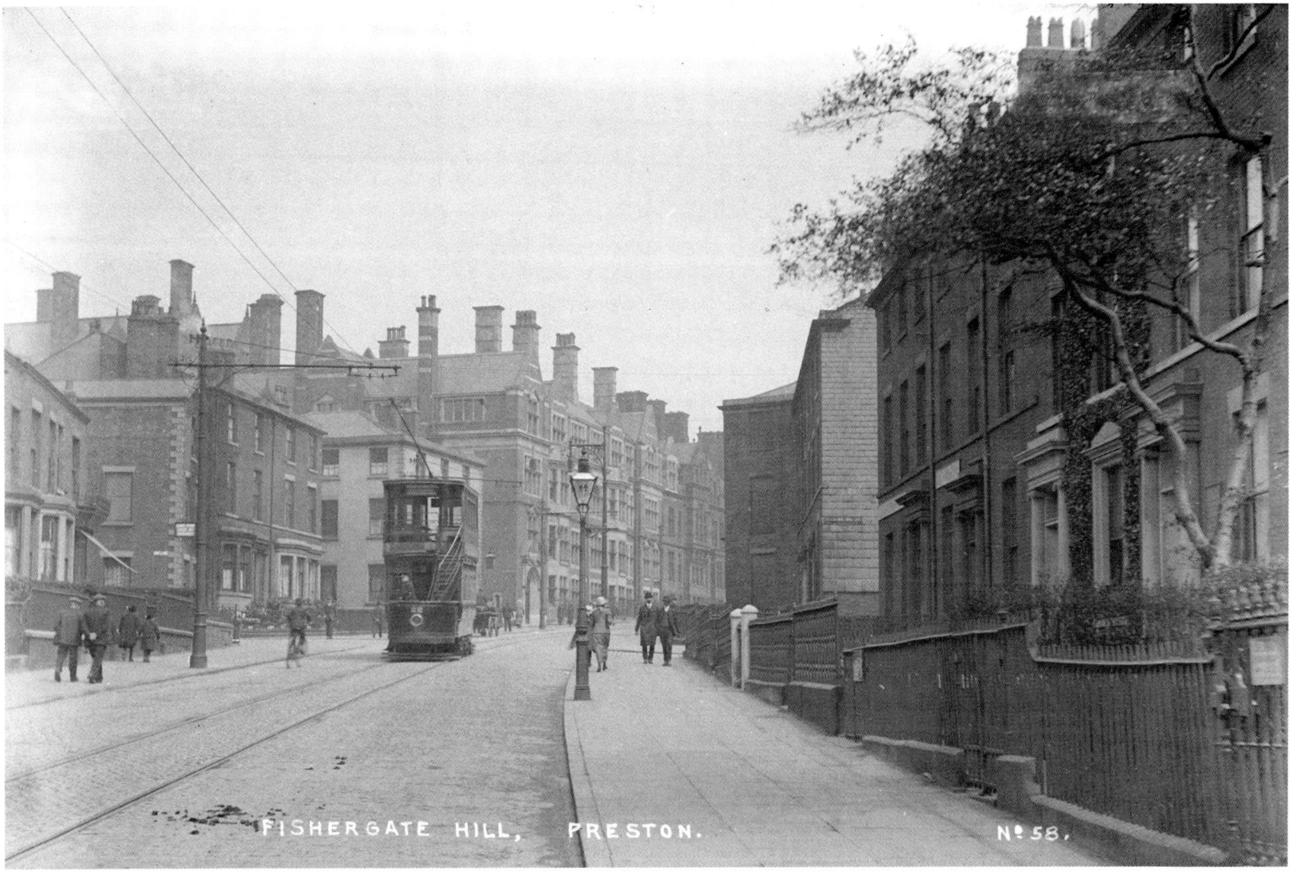

Fishergate Hill near Bow Lane.

A tram car hauls itself up Fishergate Hill from Penwortham Old Bridge, past Bow Lane and towards a magnificent range of buildings, the County Offices. This headquarters of the County Council was formally opened on September 14, 1882, further enlarged in 1895 and again in 1909. Its Fishergate frontage is faced with red brick and Minerva stone from Welsh quarries, and has monumental gables with the arms of the County Palatine, the red rose of Lancashire, and the Prince of Wales' feathers. It was designed by Henry Littler, architect to Lancashire County Council, 1896-1926, in which capacity he also designed the Sessions House in Market Square. Just beyond the two gentlemen on the right is Walton's Parade, named after a family that had owned the land since the 16th century. The last of the line, Henry Crane Walton, died at his house in Walton's Parade on February 25, 1891. Walton was a stockbroker and auctioneer who, his obituary tells us, brought about *'a very great change in the method of disposing of public properties. Formerly, vendors were subjected to additional expense through having to provide large quantities of vinous liquors, which were consumed by the habitués of the sales, which were held in the different hotels in the town. In some cases, the bills resulting from this system were very heavy indeed. Mr Walton incurred a large share of unpopularity from certain circles of bibulous people, in consequence of his decision to have his sales within his own premises. His action, however, found favour in the eyes of the public, and has since been followed in most towns'*. The splendid houses on the right were owned by a doctor, plumber, a school, a J.P., a shopman, an engineer, a bank cashier, and other private individuals.

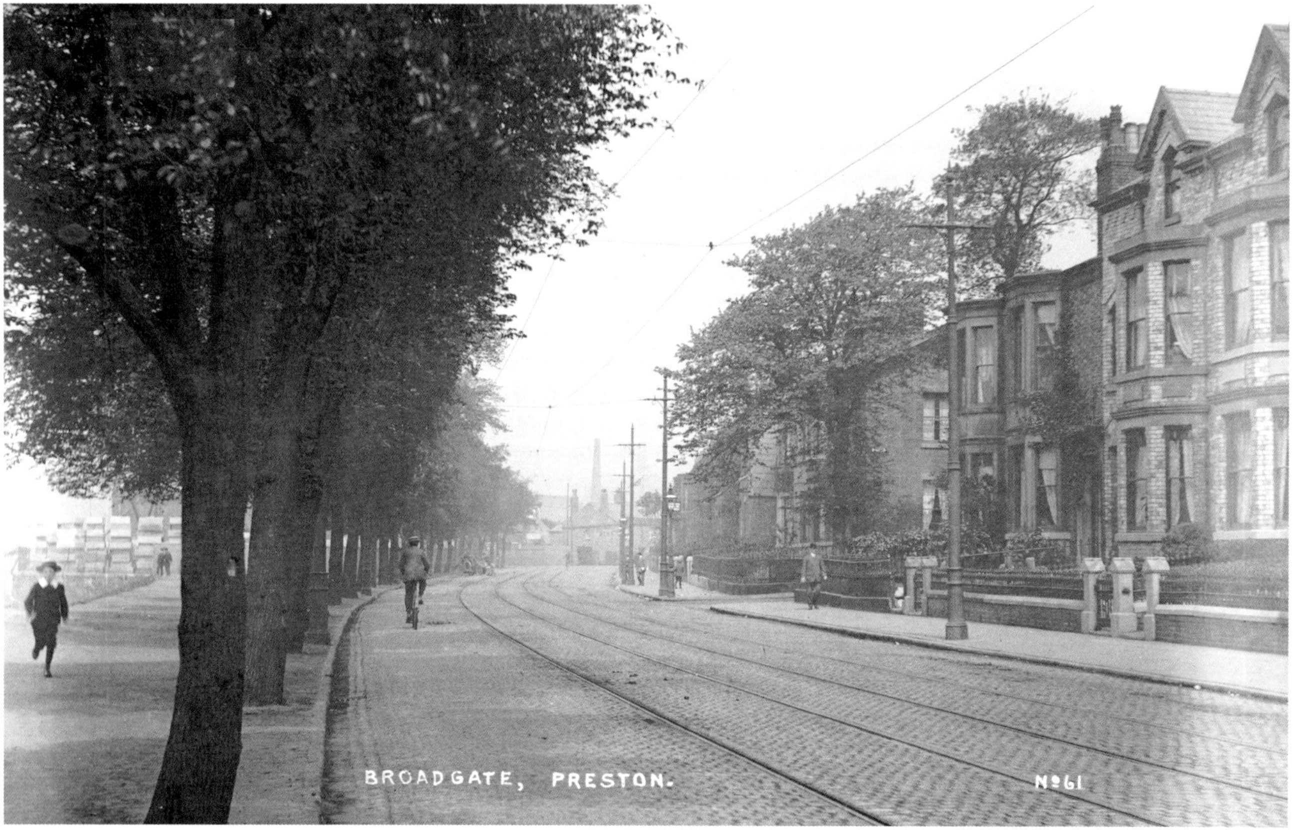

Broadgate looking towards Fishergate Hill.

Fishergate Hill and this swathe of land to the left is identified in an historical novel, *Rob Roy*, written by Sir Walter Scott and set in the time immediately preceding the Jacobite Rebellion of 1715:-*'At length we were cooped up by a superior force in the little town of Preston. We defended ourselves resolutely for one day. On the next the hearts of our leaders failed, and they resolved to surrender at discretion. To yield myself up on such terms were to have laid my head on the block. About twenty or thirty gentlemen were of my mind. We mounted our horses, and placed my daughter, who insisted on sharing my fate, in the centre of our little party. My companions, struck with her courage and filial piety, declared they would rather die than leave her behind. We rode in a body down a street called Fishergate, which leads to a marshy ground or meadow, extending to the River Ribble, through which one of our party promised to show us a good ford. This marsh had not been strongly invested by the enemy, so that we had only an affair with a patrol of Honeywood's dragoons, whom we dispersed and cut to pieces. We crossed the river, gained the high road to Liverpool, and then dispersed to seek several places of concealment and safety'.* Scott had done his homework, or knew the place personally. At that time there were three fords across the wide flat valley of Penwortham Holme; the nearest bridge was upstream at Walton. Beyond the cyclist is a car at right angles in the road which seems to be giving trouble to its owners and has caught the attention of two men across the road, to such an extent that one of them looks as if he is going to walk into the lamp-post!. The building at the end of Broadgate is the *Regatta Inn*, an old hostelry which stood at the bottom of Fishergate Hill to welcome travellers across the ford referred to in *Rob Roy*.

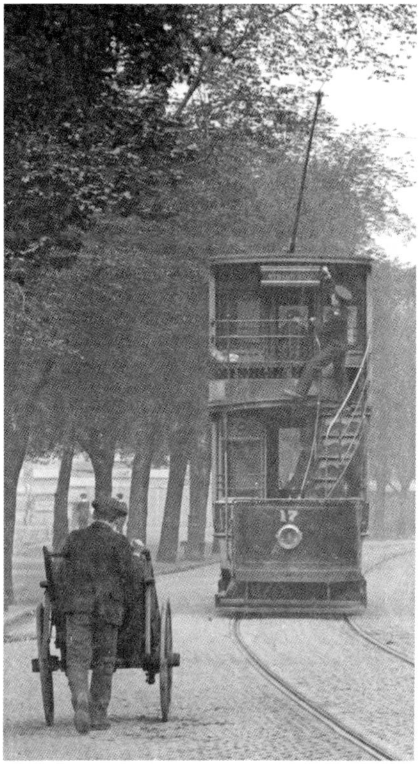

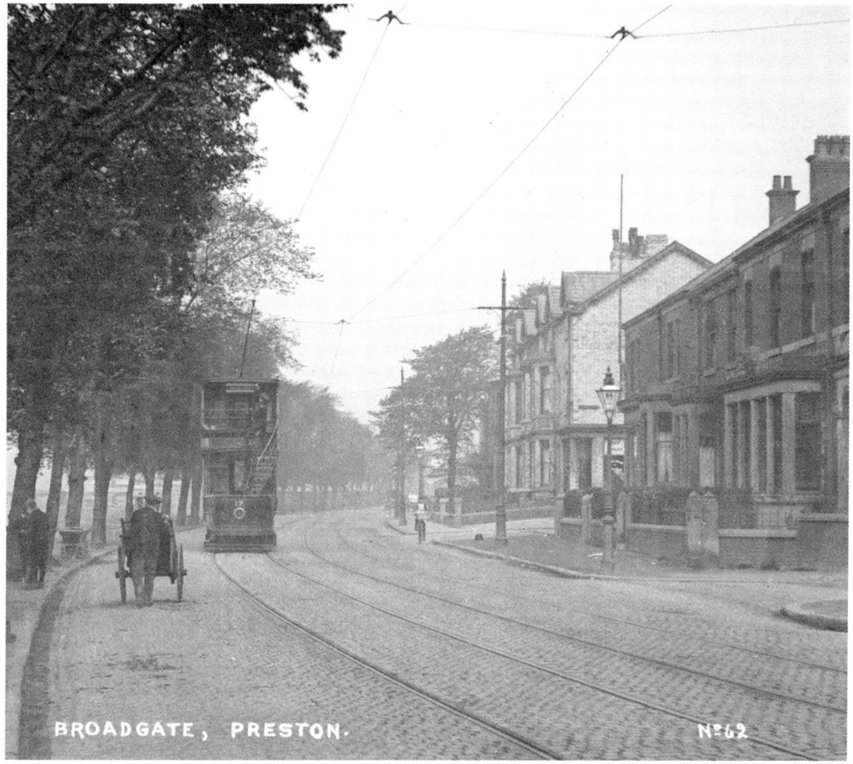

Broadgate with a tram

A conductor reaches up to adjust the destination display on his tram as it proceeds along Broadgate, which was a leafy and secluded retreat for the middling-rich in Preston at the start of the 20th century. Preston's electric tramway system opened on June 7, 1904, when 30 open-top tram cars began to run on the streets, having been purchased from the Dick, Kerr works on Strand Road, Preston, which was one of the world's leading tramcar suppliers, and which also constructed the Preston tramway system whose routes ultimately totalled 10.53 miles. The tramcars were painted in maroon and cream, with PRESTON CORPORATION TRAMWAYS in gold lettering on the side panels and the town's crest above. The livery also included ornate gold lining on the side panels and dashes, and the interiors displayed varnished woodwork, intricately crafted. The tramcar is No. 17, one of Preston's original electric trams. Then its top deck had been open to the skies; but by the time this photograph was taken, it had received a top cover – very necessary in this climate of ours! The top covers were purchased from the Strand Road works between 1907 and 1913, the works by that time bearing the name of the *United Electric Car Company*. The covers were practical, but ungainly looking, and still left the stairs and platforms open to the elements, so that there was no protection for the tram crew or for passengers boarding and alighting. One of the perennial problems with the tramway system in Preston was that whereas roads such as Broadgate, in outlying areas and carrying only one tram service, were sufficiently wide to allow double-track to be installed, in the centre of the town, where the different routes converged, the old streets were so narrow that it was only possible to provide single-track sections with passing loops at intervals to allow trams travelling in opposite directions to pass one another. This led to tramway congestion problems. When he composed his picture, the photographer may have wished to contrast the man pushing the hand-cart with the new method of transport, the electric tram; but now, ninety years later, it is the tram which somehow looks the more antiquated of the two!

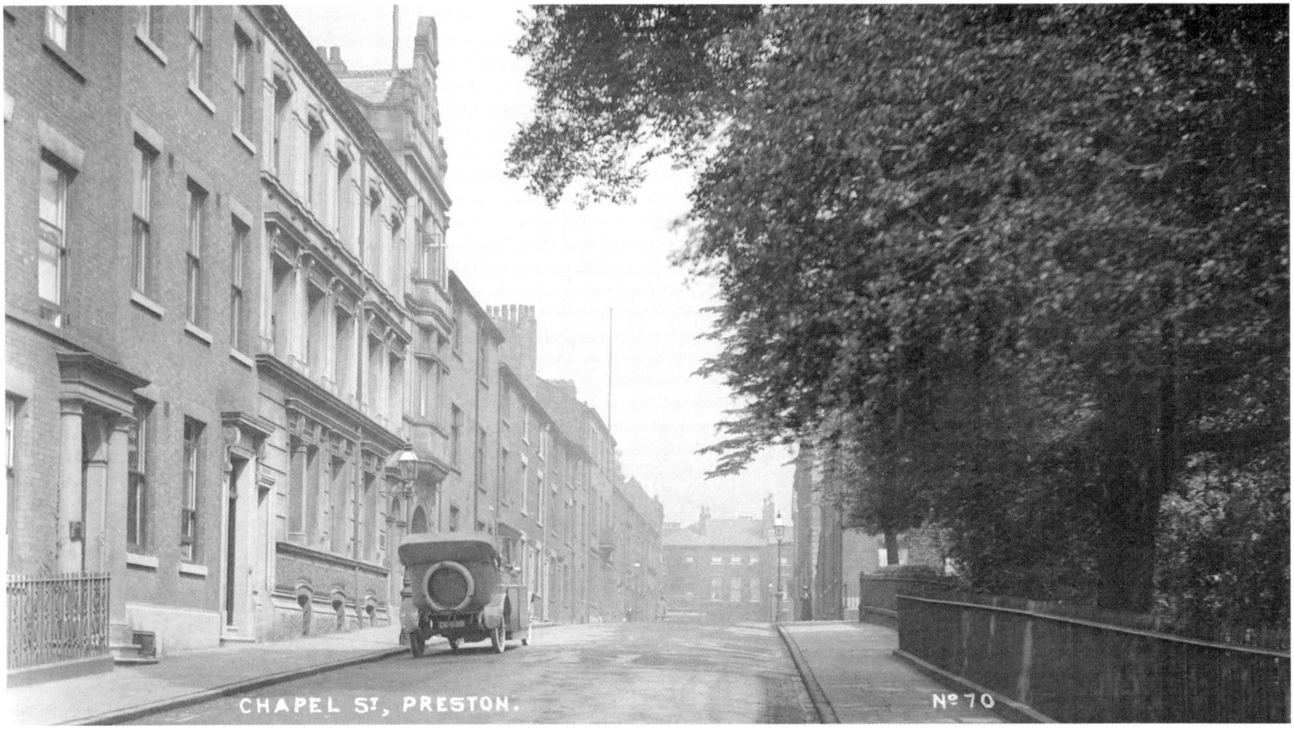

Chapel Street, Winckley Square.

Even now, some ninety years after this photograph was taken, Winckley Square retains much of its Georgian charm from the days when it housed the rich and powerful of Preston. Just visible on the right beyond the trees is the former home of Richard Newsham, banker and cotton-mill owner, whose father, John, also a banker, made his huge fortunes by striking a deal with John Horrocks, the founder of the great cotton empire of Horrockses, Crewdson & Co. After trying several bankers with no success, a desperate Horrocks approached John Newsham, who said he would match whatever he could find £1 for £1, and went on to collect his proportionate (or is it disproportionate!) share of the profits. On the left at 38, Winckley Square, is the new Catholic College building of 1898, complete with an elaborate Dutch gable on the roof line. The original Catholic College had opened at No. 27 in 1865. Living at 28, Winckley Square when this picture was taken, was Edith Rigby, wife of Charles Rigby, a local surgeon and physician. Mrs. Rigby was an ardent supporter of women's rights, and was instrumental in forming the Preston branch of the Suffragettes about 1910. On one occasion, two of the members gatecrashed a political meeting in the Public Hall, chained themselves to the seats shouting *'Votes for Women'*; one of them was Edith Rigby. They were sneered at and mocked, but they had made their point. A day or two later, visitors to Miller Park discovered that the sculpture of the 14th Earl of Derby, which stands overlooking the Terrace, had been tarred from head to feet, with a placard at its base, VOTES FOR WOMEN. Nobody owned up, but there was one lady who lived a couple of minutes walk from it – Edith Rigby. In a deserted street, a private motor vehicle – a two-seater 15.9 Darracq – coloured French grey and with the Preston registration plate CK637, marks the dawning of a new age. It was registered on March 20, 1911, in the name of Charles Sutton Jones of Frenchwood House, Preston. By February 26, 1912, it had another owner, Hubert Henry Edmondson, of 64, Fishergate, Preston. But, from the date of the photograph, it is more likely that Mr. Jones had left it here. Who would have thought that nearly a century later the same stretch of road would carry the descendants of this vehicle bumper to bumper during rush hour?

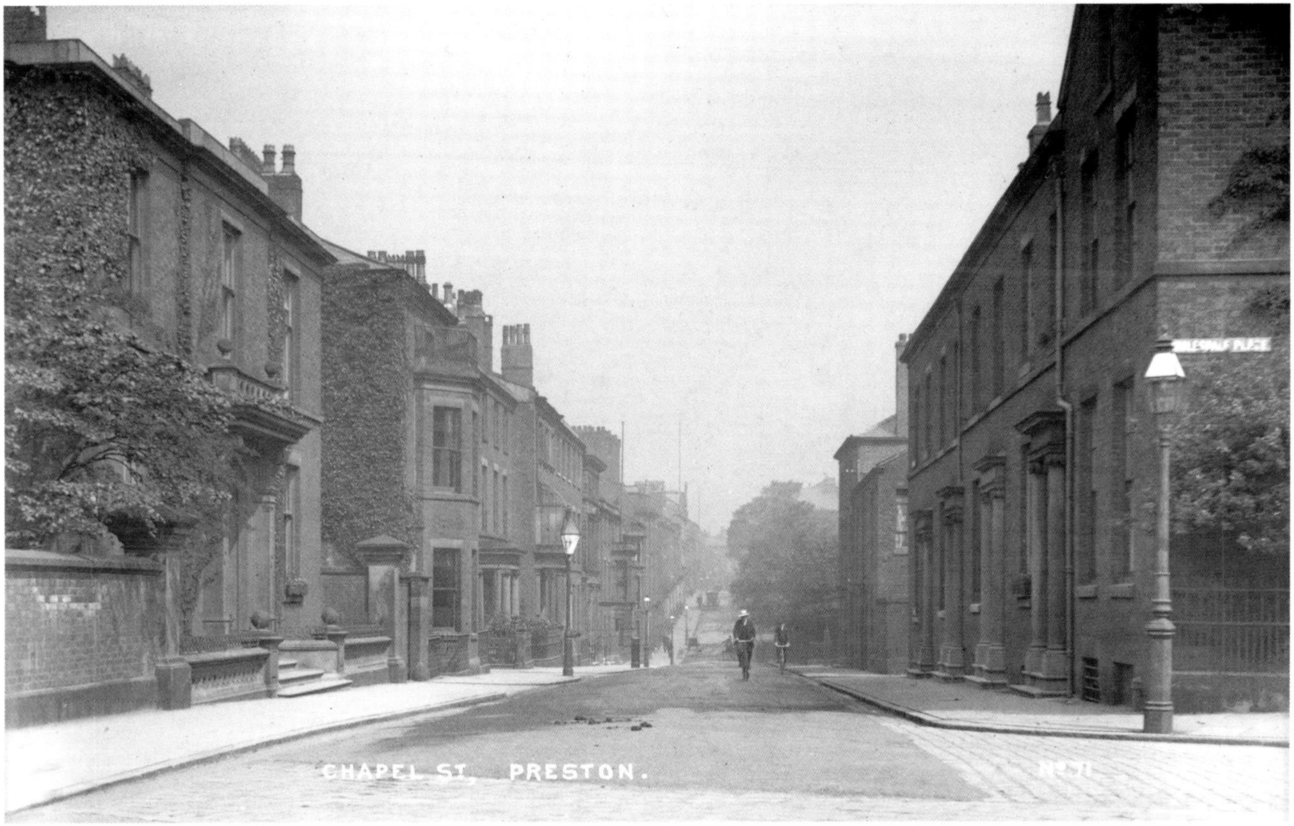

Chapel Street from Ribblesdale Place.

Chapel Street is named, not after St. Wilfrid's Chapel as most people think, but after an Independent Chapel which stood on the west corner of Chapel Street with Fishergate. Built in 1790, it ceased to be a place of worship in 1825 when its congregation moved to new premises in Cannon Street. The old chapel vanished from memory until on September 7, 1859, workmen discovered human remains from a cemetery where it had stood. Winckley Square itself is named after the family of Thomas Winckley, a Preston attorney who had owned the original parcel of land called *Town End Field*. It was progressively built on from 1801 onwards, with residences for the great and the good of Preston, including Thomas Miller, the cotton lord who gave Miller Park to the town, and Richard Newsham, whose munificent bequest of 19th century British paintings is the nucleus of the art collection in the Harris Museum and Art Gallery. Along the length of Chapel Street we see cycle power, horse power (literally), and the new motor power.

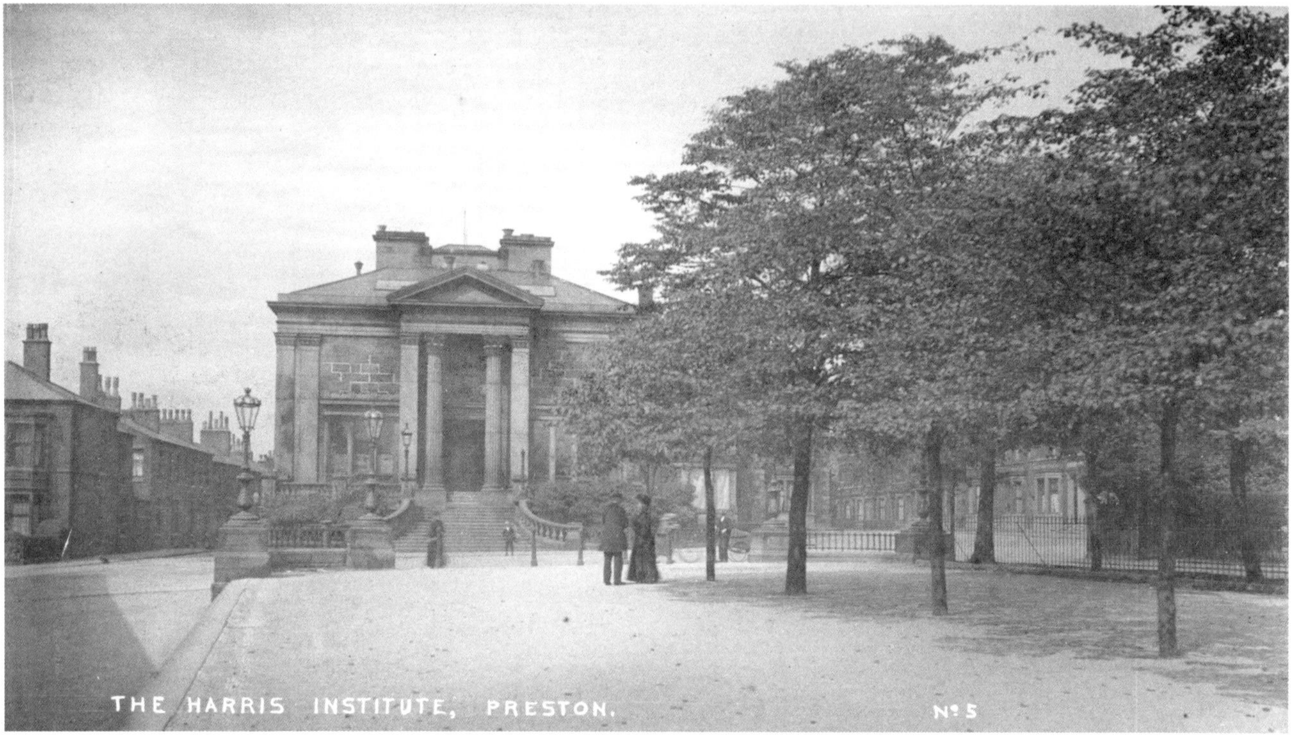

Avenham Institute, Top Walks.

A gentleman and a lady pause in conversation on Avenham Walk, a terrace overlooking the Ribble valley, which has been used as a public promenade ever since it was purchased by Preston Corporation in 1697. Immediately to the left is a steep grass slope, now part of Avenham Park, which in the early 19th century was a kitchen garden stocked with cabbages. At the foot of the slope, where the path now leads down to the tram bridge, there was a cinder track. Boys and girls used to dare each other to leap from the Walk down to the path below, damaging the angle stones at the top when they climbed back again. When the new terrace was built, the garden became neglected, and relapsed into a field, only taking on its present appearance when Avenham Park was constructed in the 1860s. But long before that, in the 1760s, it was owned by John Smalley, who collaborated with Richard Arkwright in the development of the *Water-Frame*, the first practicable spinning machine, and obtained for him the use of Arkwright House in Stonygate, formerly the residence of the headmaster of the Grammar School, to try out the new invention. But to construct and perfect it needed money, and that was found when John Smalley sold this piece of land. This is important, for it is often said that Arkwright obtained the funds for his experiments from outside the town. But no, it was Preston *'brass'* – John Smalley's money, obtained from the sale of this field – that paid for them. Arkwright was later to treat Smalley very shabbily, paying him off with a pittance for all his efforts and even forcing him to sign a document which stipulated that he would not set up in competition against him anywhere in England. *'But he forgot Wales'*, recalled Smalley, who established the *Holywell Twist Company* and went on to make a fortune of his own. And it all began with this field! Facing Avenham Walk (or *Top Walks* as it is popularly known) is the former Avenham Institute, built in 1847-49 as the successor of a Mechanics Institute which had opened in Cannon Street in 1828. Following a bequest of £40,000 by E.R. Harris in 1881, it changed its name to the Harris Institute. In 1897 it amalgamated with the newly built Harris Technical College in Corporation Street, forming an educational institution which is the early ancestor of the University of Central Lancashire.

Avenham Park and Miller Park with Ivy Bridge

In 1861, a correspondent of the Builder magazine asked: *'When will Preston think it good to make a people's park?'* He was unaware that Edward Milner, landscape gardener and chief designer to Joseph Paxton at the Crystal Palace Exhibition in 1851, had been instructed to prepare plans to convert a vast natural ampitheatre into a public park. With that aim, the land had been stealthily acquired by Preston Corporation over the years; Avenham Walk was purchased as early as 1697; six acres of land, formerly *Jackson's Garden*, in 1844; a plot of land extending Avenham Walk to its present position, from Sir Edward Stanley, in 1845; and the land fronting the park at Avenham Walk, from Mrs Cross of Redscar, in 1848. In 1850, Preston Corporation withdrew its opposition to

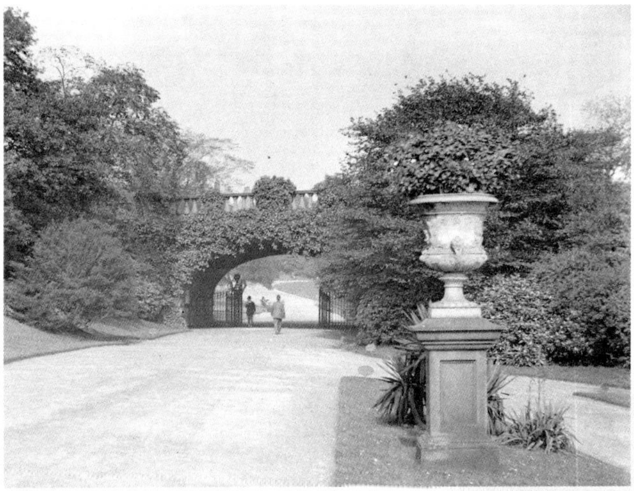

the East Lancashire Railway crossing the river at this spot because the company agreed to construct a public path across the bridge and to make the embankment slopes flatter to harmonise with the natural incline of the park. In 1851, all the land extending from the river, including the land shown here, was purchased from a Lieutenant Colonel Cross. The jig-saw was complete when the tramway owned by the Lancaster Canal Company, which extended from the Old Tram Bridge and through the outer rim of the parkland to Chapel Street, ceased to operate in 1859. The two parks were constructed by out-of-work cotton operatives in 1864-67, when the American Civil War caused a stoppage in the supply of cotton, and threw large numbers out of work. As they said at the time, *'out of seeming evil good has been educed, and the 'ills' have fallen, for 'gracious ends''*. Even as these notes are being written, steps are being taken to restore this magnificent park illustrated below, along with the adjacent Miller Park, to its former glory.

Miller Park, on the left, occupies eleven acres between two railway embankments. Its boundary with Avenham Park, to the east, is marked by *'Ivy Bridge'* over which the trains of the East Lancashire Railway Company passed on their way to Southport. The bridge, named retrospectively after the ivy which festoons its entire structure, has been given a picturesque balustrade to create the impression of a walkway in the grounds of a country mansion. Only when the whistle screamed and a steam locomotive appeared on the bridge were visitors to the park aware that it was a railway line. Originally the parks had wrought iron gates at their entrances and at their boundary at the bridge. Who knows, one day they may be replaced. An early description of the railway embankment on the left, tells us that the trees *'have made rapid progress since the time they were planted. Among them are elms, limes, birch, pinus Austriaca, hollys of various sorts, yews, and ligistrum of different kinds'*. To the right there were *'choice specimens of pines, including cembra excelsa, lumbertiana, thuya lobi, and Chinese juniper'*.

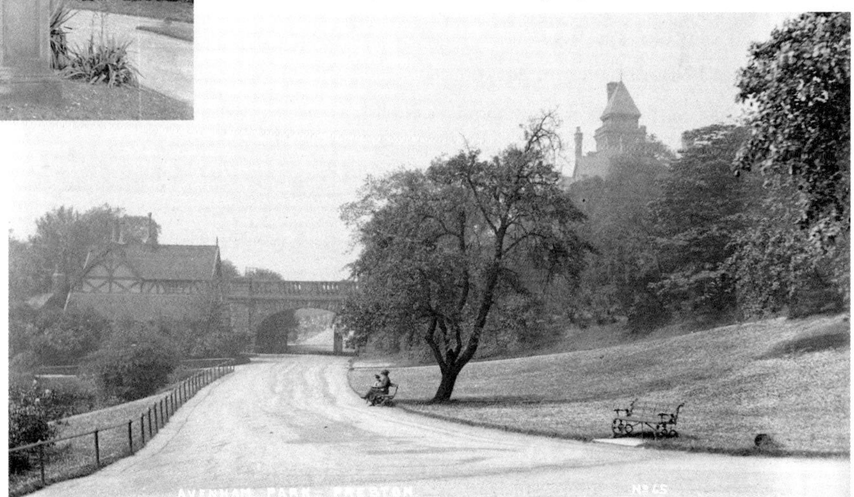

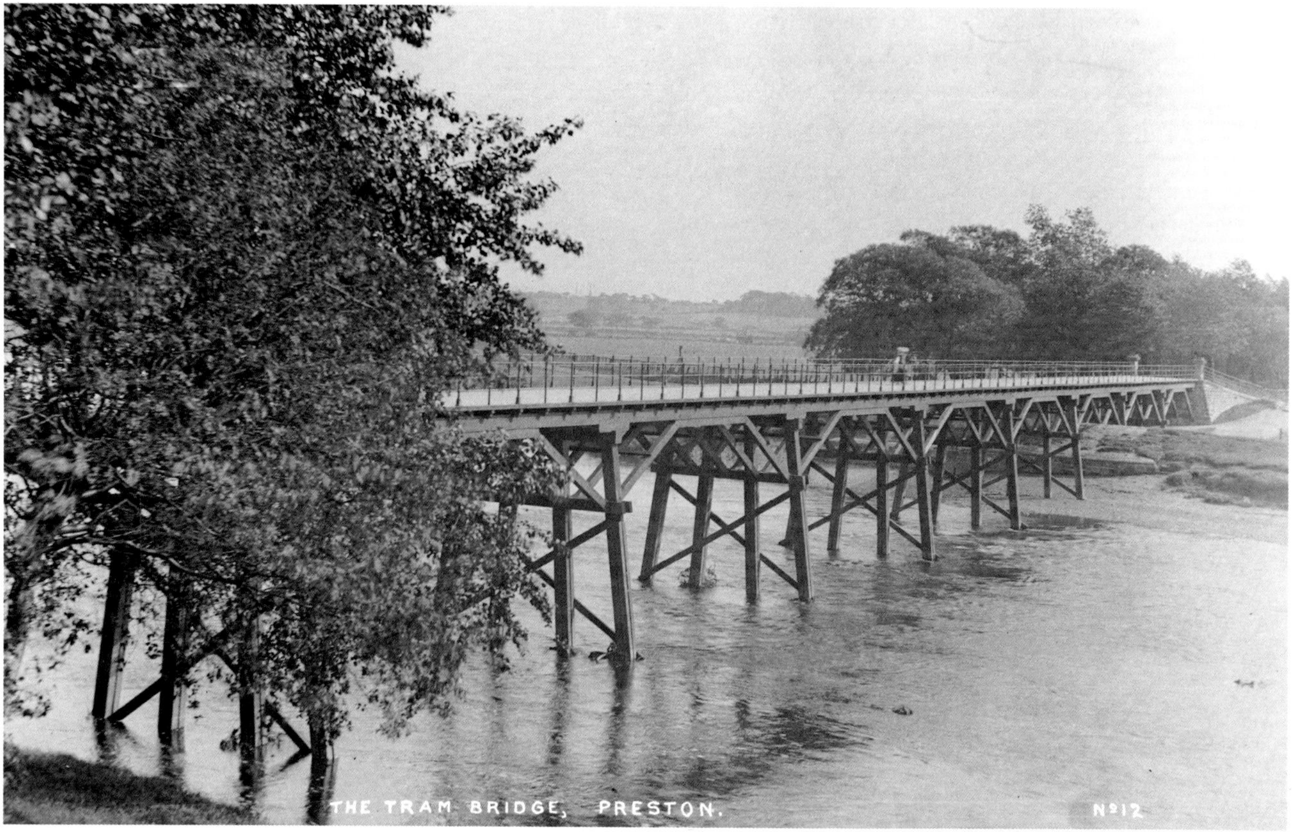

The Old Tram Bridge, Avenham Park.

In February 1864, the Council resolved *'that the road between the two railwy bridges under the Cliff be proceeded with; that the walks and plantations at Avenham Park, below the tramway be proceeded with, and that the buildings in Wise's and Jackson's gardens be pulled down'*. As early as 1798, canal communication between Preston and Burton-in-Westmoreland was established; this was extended from Preston to Wigan in 1802. An integral part of this canal system was the Old Tramway Bridge, shown here in the photograph as it looked after a late 19th century reconstruction but long before the present sympathetic concrete imitation supplanted it in the late 1950s. The tramway comprised two lines of cast-iron rails which carried wagons between the Preston terminus of the Lancaster Canal (which extended to a spot near the junction of Corporation Street and the Penwortham Bypass) and the southern section at Walton Summit. Only now, 200 years later, has the plan to join the two sections of canal together been realised, at last giving access to the countrywide canal network which was originally envisaged. The old tramway ceased to run in 1859, and a steam engine which had been used to hoist the wagons up the 1 in 6 gradient, and which stood on the site of the flagpole, was demolished in 1868. Interestingly, John Proctor, the last driver of the tramway, made two journeys a day, there and back, from Preston to Walton Summit for 32 years. Proctor, like all drivers, was not allowed to ride on the wagons, and it is said that he had to get his clogs resoled every week! Near to this spot is a fountain at *'Stone Delph'*; it was supplied at that time by the waters of a spring of *'excellent water'* that *'never abates in either summer or winter'*. Previously, it had been *'allowed to run away, and it was conveyed in an old wooden trough to the river, near the stone delph'*.

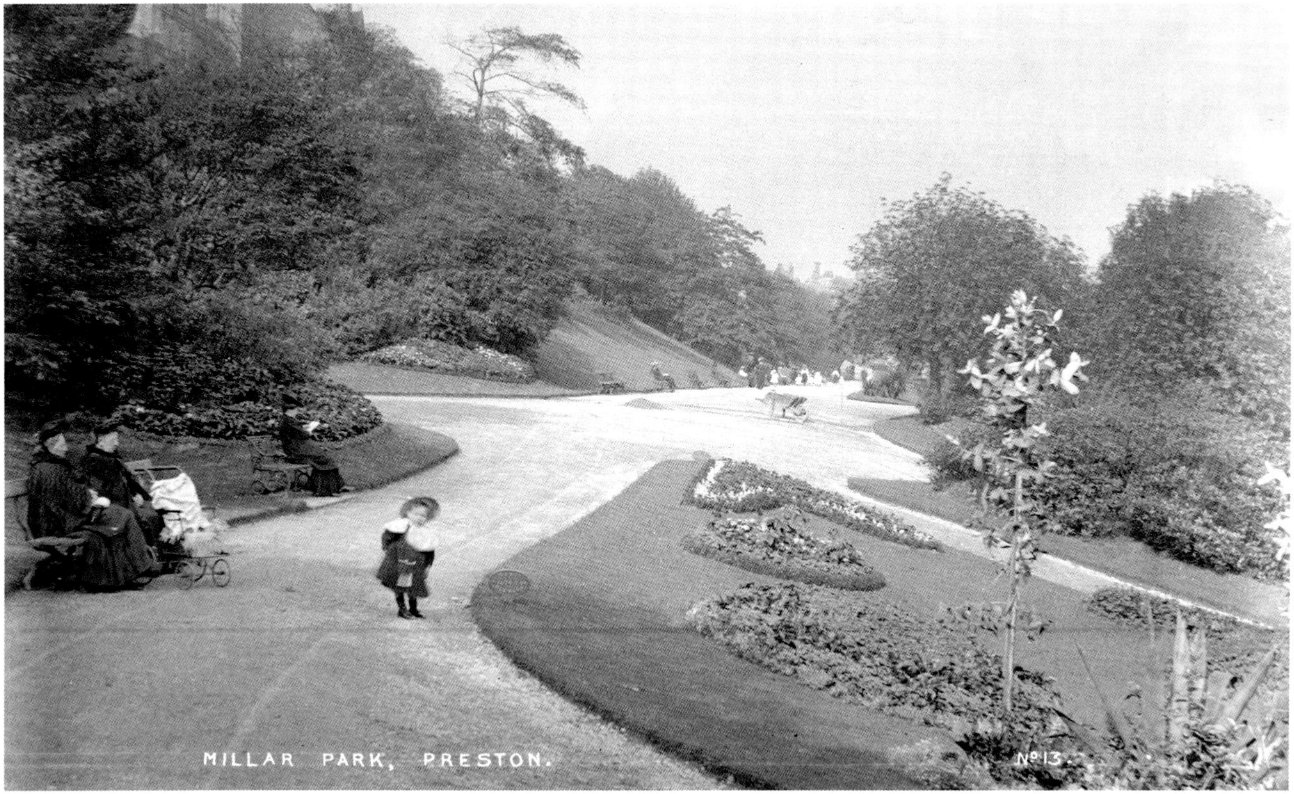

Miller Park.

This photograph shows the west end of the terrace, the principal unifying ornamental feature of Miller Park. An writer describes it as *'24 feet wide, and ornamented on the southern side with six architectural stone piers, surmounted by artistically designed vases, filled with geraniums and fuschias, which have a very charming effect for several months during the summer. Ascending the steps on the north of the terrace there is observed a rosary, consisting of nine beds filled with choice varieties of roses, chiefly the hybrid perpetuals'*. To the left, the path branches away towards West Cliff, which comes out at Fishergate Hill; and to the right, which leads through the archway of the old North Union railway bridge to Broadgate. According to Victorian writers, '*Miller Park may be regarded as a continuation, westward, of Avenham Park*'. And yet the two are laid out in such radically contrasting styles; Avenham Park retains all the qualities of a natural landscape, whilst Miller Park is a wonderful combination of artificial features, - a terrace, fountain, and carefully constructed paths such as those surrounding the neat flower beds seen here in the foreground. Even the former Park Hotel, seen rising over the tree-covered slopes, was placed on a central axis overlooking the park. All the more astonishing that it was one designer, Edward Milner, who had also been called on to improve Moor Park, who was responsible for both designs. Miller Park was named after Alderman Thomas Miller, Jnr., who presented the land to the Corporation in 1864. But Miller never saw his dream realised; he died in 1865, and both Avenham and Miller Parks were opened in 1867. Here in the foreground we see two stern-faced matriarchs resting on a park bench. With them is a young child who has left his pram to get a closer look at the photographer; beyond them, a woman catches up with some reading. The fashions may have changed, but such scenes are familiar in Preston's parks to the present day.

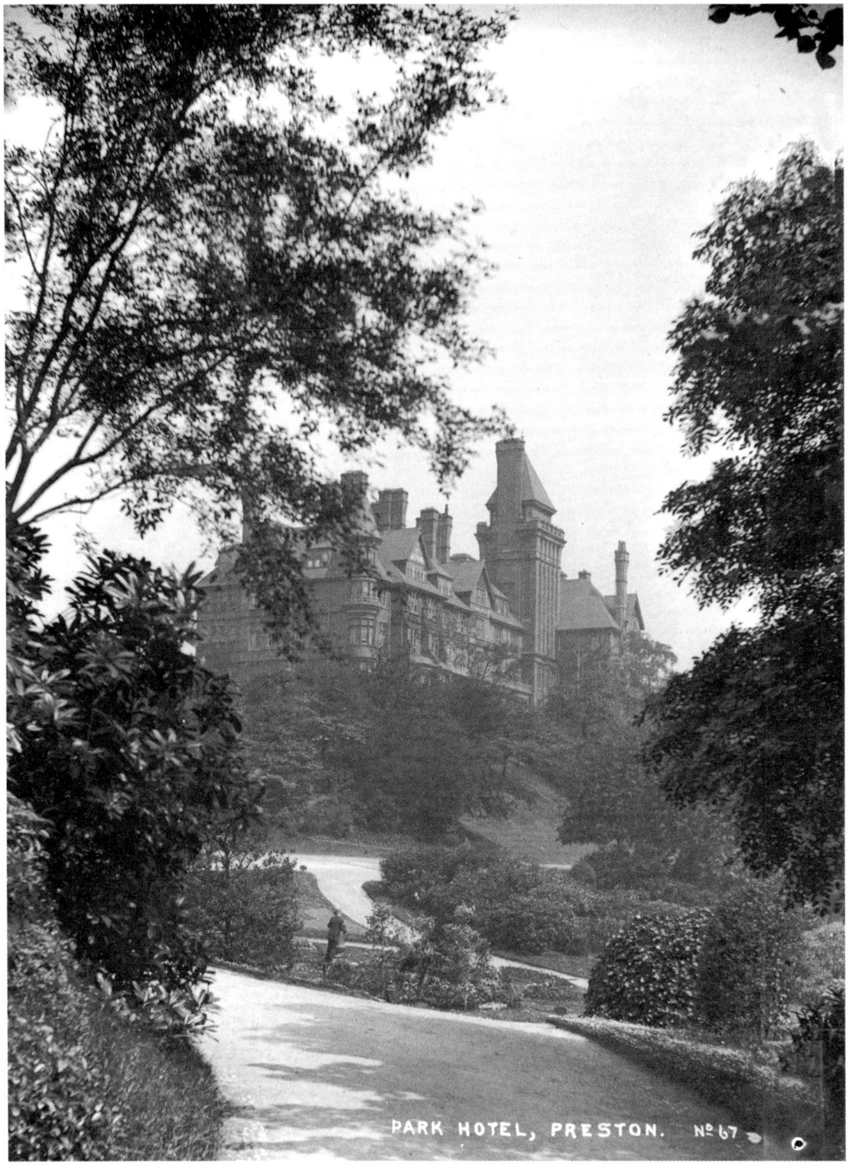

The Park Hotel, Miller Park.

This splendid photograph must be one of the most beautiful ever to have been taken of the former Park Hotel (now offices belonging to Lancashire County Council) in Miller Park. For Victorian and Edwardian passengers approaching Preston by rail the Park Hotel took on the guise of a magnificent mansion set in its own landscape garden. It was designed by the Oldham architect, Arnold Mitchell, for the London and North-Western and Lancashire and Yorkshire Railway Companies. Built in red Ruabon brick with a red tiled roof, it has a frontage over Miller Park of 174 feet, with a tower that rises to a height of 113 feet 9 inches. Shortly after it was built, it was described as *'fine, massive, stately and picturesque; but in colour the structure looks too red: age will, however, tone it down considerably in this respect; while familiarity with the building will wear-off what at first sight has an incongruous appearance in the higher or surmounting part – the close contiguity of a chimney or ventilating shaft with the tower'*. But internally it had all the then *'mods and cons'* – *'drawing, dining, breakfast, commercial, writing, billiard, smoking and other rooms; while for sleeping purposes it contains a large number of rooms, with bath, lavatory, and other accommodation attached'*. For the guests at the south front of the hotel, there was *'a charming view of Miller and Avenham Parks, the Ribble Valley, and the distant hills filling up the south-eastern horizon'*. The view shown here has been marred by an intrusive office extension of the 1960s, which now obscures the western side of the building.